THE
TRUTHS
WE MUST
BELIEVE

THE
TRUTHS
WE MUST
BELIEVE

Dr. Chris Thurman

THOMAS NELSON PUBLISHERS
Nashville

Copyright © 1991 by Chris Thurman

Published in Nashville, Tennessee, by Thomas Nelson, Inc., and distributed in Canada by Lawson Falle, Ltd., Cambridge, Ontario.

Scripture quotations are from the NEW KING JAMES VERSION of the Bible. Copyright © 1979, 1980, 1982, Thomas Nelson, Inc., Publishers.

Scripture quotations marked NIV are taken from The Holy Bible: New International Version. Copyright © 1978 by the New York International Bible Society. Used by permission of Zondervan Bible Publishers.

ISBN 0-8407-7659-4

Printed in the United States of America

1 2 3 4 5 6 7—96 95 94 93 92 91

To . . .

My wife, Holly. When we married, I vowed to love and cherish you forever. After eleven years of marriage, I can only say . . . forever isn't long enough.

My children, Matthew, Ashley, and Kelly. Your lives have helped me rediscover the joy and excitement of life. I pray that I will be a dad who lives truth in front of you, not one who just talks it. You are so precious to me.

CONTENTS

■

PART THREE: DOING THE TRUTH, FINDING ULTIMATE TRUTH

ACKNOWLEDGEMENTS

■

This book could not have been written without the kind support of a number of people. I would like to take a moment to acknowledge them for their invaluable help.

I appreciate all the many ways the staff of the Minirth-Meier Clinic in Richardson, Texas, supported me during the six years I was there. Special thanks to Dr. Frank Minirth and Dr. Paul Meier for providing me so many different professional opportunities that allowed me to grow as a psychologist. Thanks also to the staff at my current professional home, the Minirth-Meier Tunnell and Wilson Clinic of Austin. They have made my transition from Dallas to Austin a very smooth and enjoyable one. I look forward to many years of working with them to serve the needs of hurting people.

The staff at Thomas Nelson Publishers, as usual, has been fantastic. I cannot imagine a publishing company that does more for its authors than Thomas Nelson. My special thanks to Janet Thoma who has been with me from the start of my efforts as an author. Her constant support and guidance were always a source of encouragement as I tried to put into words the many ideas that bang around in my mind. Many thanks, also, to Susan Salmon for her insight and sensitivity in the final editing of this book. She was extremely helpful in polishing the ideas presented herein. Last, but certainly not least, I owe tremendous thanks to Dr. Dennis Hensley for helping me take this book from a rather rough initial draft to a polished final version. A well known author and lecturer, Dr. Hensley was a godsend in the numerous ways he took what I had to say and made it much better. He added many fine touches to this book, something that I will always be indebted to him for. Thanks, Dennis, for all your hard work.

I am deeply indebted to the many patients who allowed me to take an intimate look inside their lives. They have shown me what courage is all about as they attempted to face the truth and grow into mature adults. I owe them more than they know, and I will never be the same for having been allowed the privilege of working with them.

Authors often thank their spouses for the support and encouragement they offer during the trials and tribulations of writing a book. My wife, Holly, is no exception. I cannot tell you the myriad of ways she lovingly supported me as this book was written. The many times I felt stuck in a certain section of the book or confused as to how to express something or fearful that the book was not turning out like I wanted it to, she was there with the words of encouragement that I needed to hear. Holly, thanks for who you are and how you add so much to my life. You are truly a gift from God.

My utmost thanks are to God for who He is and for how He is always there loving and challenging me. As I move through my third decade of life, I feel like I am just beginning to more fully grasp what He is all about and what He wants me to be all about. God is love, something He has certainly proved over and over again to me. God is also truth. If this book has any truth in it, and it is my fervent hope that it is full of truth, it is God working through someone as unworthy as me in His efforts to help you become a mature human being, complete and lacking nothing. I hope and pray that is exactly how He uses this book in your life.

Chris Thurman, Ph.D.
Austin, Texas
August 1991

INTRODUCTION

■

I have been trained as a psychologist to encourage patients to avoid using the word *must* in their vocabulary. The primary reason is that the word *must* suggests a lack of freedom to choose and tends to create feelings of being trapped rather than seeing that we do have choices in life. Acknowledging our freedom to choose and taking responsibility for our choices is critically important for mental health. So we psychologist types encourage patients to avoid saying "I must . . ." and to replace it with statements like "I choose . . ." or "I want to . . ." or "It would be best for me if I . . .".

With all that said, it is somewhat strange that I would end up titling this book, *The Truths We* Must *Believe*. It is as if I am suggesting we have no choice but to believe certain truths, when, in fact, I know that we do have a great deal of choice in deciding what to believe and what not to believe. Frankly, we can believe anything we want in life!

Yet let me challenge you. I purposely chose the title of this book because I wanted to make something clear to you before you even read the first word of the first chapter. What I want to make clear is this: In order to be emotionally healthy, we *must* believe certain truths. There is no choice in the matter; emotional health is obtained via certain truths. Without these truths fully understood, accepted, and put to use, there is no emotional health.

So despite my early training as a psychologist, I do believe that the word *must* has an appropriate place in our efforts to overcome emotional problems. I certainly agree that we have the freedom to believe whatever we want. But I believe there are certain truths we must believe or we will never be truly emotionally healthy people. It is like physical health. We don't have to be physically healthy, but if we want to be, we must diet, exercise, and rest. Physical health cannot be obtained any other way. Similarly, we don't have to be mentally healthy during our trip through life, but if we want to be, we must believe and practice the truth. There is no other way.

In this book, I will share with you twelve truths that I contend we "must" believe if we are to become emotionally healthy. Other psychologists, I'm sure, would suggest a list different from mine, but the twelve truths I explore are among the most important that you will ever come face to face with in life. Study them carefully. Honestly ask whether you really believe them or not. Honestly examine whether or not you practice them in your life. And at the end of the book, I will ask you to honestly examine who the source of these truths is.

Take the truths discussed in this book as seriously as you can, for they will dictate your emotional health and the quality of your life. They are that important. As William Lloyd Garrison once stated, "In proportion as we perceive and embrace the truth we do become just, heroic, magnanimous, divine."

PART ONE

■

TRUTH
AND
EMOTIONAL
HEALTH

CHAPTER 1

■

The Absolute Necessity of Truth for an Emotionally Healthy Life

All truth is an achievement.
—Munger

Men don't usually like to reveal their deeper feelings. When they finally decide they can't keep things to themselves any longer they often seek out another man to "talk things over with."

But when the problem runs really deep—deep enough to threaten their personal stability—they will bypass their golf buddies, work cohorts, and even their best friends. Instead, they turn to someone like me. I'm a listener. A professional listener.

Bill needed a listener. He called for an appointment and came to my office on a hot July afternoon. He dropped into an armchair and combed his fingers through his hair. His eyes were bloodshot. The fresh nicks on his face were indicative of the hit-and-miss shave he had given himself that morning. There were bags under his eyes. He had that haggard look of a man too exhausted to keep trying, yet too terrified to close his eyes in sleep.

"How may I help you?" I asked.

Bill was quiet for a few seconds, expecting me to say more. Instead, I just eased back in my chair and waited. Whatever he needed to talk about I knew he had rehearsed dozens of times before ever phoning me. I'd let him explain in his own time, in his own way.

"I'm losing it," he finally blurted out. "I don't know if I'm cracking up or falling apart or what! I'm wiped out, and if I don't get myself pulled back together soon, I don't know what's going to happen to me. I need some help."

"Please go on, I'm listening."

"I've never had a time in my life like this past year," he said in a low voice. "It's like a black cloud is floating over my head all the time. I'm constantly depressed. Every day is a burden. I toss and turn at night, and I don't want to face each day. I can't seem to shake this feeling of hopelessness."

"Things seem pretty bad all the way around," I said, stating the obvious, hoping he would say more about what was bothering him.

"Yeah, everything seems pretty bleak. I thought something might be wrong with me physically, so I had our family doctor give me the once over. He couldn't find anything wrong with me. No symptoms. No headaches or stomach cramps or fevers. He thought it was stress. He talked me into trying to rest more often and get some exercise. It didn't help though. I'm still walking around like a zombie. I went back to see him again. I asked him for some sleeping pills, but he said I needed something else. He said I needed to talk to a guy like you. You know . . . a . . . a . . ."

"A listener?" I suggested.

Bill grinned ever so slightly. "Yeah, a listener."

"Well, I'm glad you decided to come. Let me ask you, was there anything that may have triggered your depression?" I asked.

"I don't know," said Bill, waving one hand limply before his face. "Just a bunch of stuff. At work . . . at home . . . it all adds up after a while."

"Tough times at work, you say?"

"Aw, yeah, work has been a real bummer since we dropped a government bid back in February. It was my project—my baby all the way. I had every angle figured. Our plans were the best. Our prices were the lowest. Our guarantees were the most dependable. Anyone with half an ounce of sense would have seen in an instant that our company should have been awarded that contract."

"But . . . ?"

"But we didn't get it. Our main competitor did, although I have no idea why. I did my best, but we lost. And losing that contract meant losing big bucks— megabucks! Millions! Years of steady work! Nobody said anything, but I had this feeling that everybody felt it was my fault, that I had blown it somehow and now everyone else was going to suffer because of my failure. I could feel their eyes on me when I went to work each day."

"Losing the contract was a big disappointment for you and your company. I take it that this isn't the first big contract that your company has lost out on."

"No, no, that's true. But it came at a time when I needed something positive in my life. I didn't need any new troubles. My son—the middle one—was having trouble in school. He's the sweetest kid you've ever met, but he just can't read very well. He's got some kind of learning disability. They've been working with him for a couple of years now, but it's slow going. He can't keep pace with the other kids his age."

Bill stood up and walked to the window, blinking back tears in an effort to appear strong. I gave him a moment of silence as he collected himself and recalled events from the previous year.

"They told us to hold our son back a grade," Bill continued, "but I resisted it. I should have listened. By midway through the next year he was way behind the other students in everything except math and physical education. My wife and I told the teacher to help him as much as she could and that we'd let him repeat that grade."

"You felt bad about that, didn't you?"

Bill nodded. "It tore the heart right out of me. The kid tried so hard, but there I was breaking the news to him that he'd be in that same grade again next year," he replied, tears again welling up in his eyes.

"It was almost as if you had failed that grade along with your son, wasn't it?"

"I failed him, that's for sure. And it came when I failed the company too."

"The double whammy," I said, trying to console him.

Bill smirked, turned from the window and moved back to his chair. "The triple whammy. My wife and I started having some marital problems about then. She started in again with this 'thing' she's always had about wanting to buy her dream home. Well, that dream home has a nightmare price tag. I put my foot in my mouth when I promised her we could buy it. I got her hopes up."

"That was back when you were certain your company was going to land the big government contract," I surmised.

"Yeah. And that would have meant a fat bonus for me and probably a raise too. We could have handled the new mortgage payments with that kind of money. But when the bonus and raise didn't materialize, my wife still wanted the new house. She had told all her friends we were going to move. She said we'd both have to eat crow if we didn't buy the bigger place."

"I assume you and your wife have discussed your financial situation?"

"Hey, I tried. Believe me, I tried. But she wasn't in a very receptive mood . . . and that's putting it mildly. I may have to go ahead and try to buy that new house if she keeps on like this. It doesn't look like I've got any other choice if I ever want peace in the family again. How I will pay for it is anybody's guess though. It's crazy. My whole life is crazy. Maybe *I'm* crazy. What do you think? Am I off my nut or what?"

I smiled reassuringly. "No, Bill, you're not crazy, just hurting and confused. You're hurting over some painful situations that would be tough for anyone to deal with. Also, you're confused about the truth of your situation."

Bill's head jerked up. His eyes narrowed as if I had just called him a liar. "Hey, I'm not making any of this stuff up. What I told you is true. I swear it!"

"Bill, I believe you're telling me the truth as best as you understand it," I suggested, "but there's a lot more truth to your circumstances than you are currently aware of. Have you ever heard the expression, 'Know the truth and the truth will set you free'?"

"Yes."

"Well, in our work together, I hope to show you just how true that statement is. Knowing the truth and being set free by it are what counseling is really all about. Here in this office, you and I are going to play our own version of 'To Tell the Truth.' We are going to find out what the real truth is about the situations troubling you. Are you willing to try?"

Bill looked a little dubious, but he shrugged his shoulders.

"Okay," he finally agreed. "Just don't turn it into 'Truth or Consequences.' I've already had enough of those to last me a lifetime."

THE CHALLENGE OF TRUTH

Thoreau once wrote, "Most men lead lives of quiet desperation." Bill was just such a man. He had spent his life feeling pushed around by emotional struggles, feeling desperate but not knowing what to do to solve the struggles. You, or someone you know, may also feel "desperate" about what to do concerning emotional turmoil related to difficult or painful situations in life. If so, this book is going to provide a great deal of help for you.

In the coming chapters I am going to teach you the truths I taught Bill, as well as hundreds of other men and women like him whom I have counseled. Additionally, I am going to show you how to put the truth to use in your life so that emotional health can be yours. The bottom line underlying all the things I will share with you in this book is this: *Dedication to know-*

BELIEVING

ing and doing the truth is the most important requirement for emotional health.

Truth is our road map for negotiating the difficult challenges of life. Without truth, we have no way of knowing how to view the things that happen to us or how to successfully move beyond them. Without truth to guide us, we get lost and develop emotional problems, which are the signs that tell us we are lost.

Unfortunately, knowing and doing the truth are far greater challenges than most of us realize. Humankind has faced these two difficulties throughout the centuries and, frankly, not fared too well. Some of the greatest thinkers of all time—Plato, Aristotle, Descartes, Hume, Locke, and countless others—have sought to understand truth and its application to life. Even Pontius Pilate asked Jesus that all important question that begs to be answered in each person's life, "What is truth?" (John 18:38). Failure to answer this one question correctly is truly failure indeed. From my own observations, relatively few people are successful in really understanding the deeper truths of life, much less in consistently applying them to their lives.

Why do we struggle so greatly in our efforts to know and do the truth? While there are many answers to that question, the primary answer is simple yet frightening. Understanding the truth and acting on it takes tremendous determination and courage, and most of us just aren't that committed. It is human nature to avoid a difficult challenge, particularly when an easy way out is available. In his book *The Road Less Traveled*, psychiatrist M. Scott Peck put it this way: "Fearing the pain involved, almost all of us, to a greater or lesser degree, attempt to avoid problems."[1]

Discovering and doing the truth are among life's toughest problems, so we often avoid them. We often settle for half-truths or no truth at all (full-blown lies) because they are usually easier to come by than the truth. They don't require as much effort to apply and to live as does the truth. It's like the college student's tendency to read the *Cliff's Notes* version of a book rather than to painfully labor through the original manuscript for a deeper understanding of what the author was trying to say. It's a shame that we do this. Settling for less than the complete truth is a bandage, not a true remedy for what emotionally ails us in life.

When poet Robert Frost wrote of a road that split into two different paths, he was warning us that the more traveled path might be easier to traverse but ultimately less satisfying and growth producing and that the less traveled path, though more difficult, ends up being the one that is more worthwhile. Each day in life we find ourselves facing this same Frostian dilemma of whether or not to follow the more difficult but healthier path of truth that few people follow or the easier but unhealthier path of lies that most people choose. Our choice each day concerning this "fork in the road" makes all the difference in how our lives turn out.

In the book *Alice's Adventures in Wonderland*, Alice came to a crossroads and asked the Cheshire cat which road she should take. "Where are you going?" asked the cat. "I don't know," answered Alice. "Oh, well," said the cat, "in that case, either road will take you there." If "there" is emotional health, then either road won't take you there. Truth is the only road to emotional health. There is no other path.

If you are interested in taking the difficult path of truth through life, there is good news, though. The good news is that truth is available to anyone who wants it, which also means that emotional health is possible for everyone. It doesn't matter if you are male or female, black or white (or any other color), young or old, American or Russian, rich or poor, educated or uneducated, from a functional or dysfunctional family. Truth does not discriminate. The further good news is that truth, when understood and applied, produces life in full, liberty from unnecessary suffering and pain, and happiness in the form of peace and contentment no matter how your life may be going. In other words, the hard work of being a person dedicated to the truth pays off handsomely.

So we don't ever need to ask, "Can I be an emotionally healthy, mature, content, self-controlled, happy, and stable person?" The answer is a resounding, "Yes!" The more honest and difficult question we need to ask ourselves is, "Do I really want to be an emotionally healthy person badly enough to pay the price for it?"

If you want to be emotionally healthy, you have quite a challenge in front of you. The effort to be a person of truth will demand more of you than anything else you will ever try to do. Anything! That is why most of us want emotional health but give up along the way in our pursuit of it. It is tough work.

Whether you realize it or not, truth is the most important issue in your life. It is more important than what you do for a living, who you are married to, or what you earn. I am convinced that truth is the bottom line of life. You cannot have "real life" without truth. A life without truth (or with only partial truth) is not much of a life at all. It contains little of the emotional health, maturity, or completeness that most of us want.

If you have reached the fork in the road where you must decide between truth and lies and you want to take the path of truth, I can provide a map and a compass to help keep you on the straight and narrow. I have had the chance to observe life through my own eyes, as you, likewise, have seen it through your eyes. However, as a psychologist I have also had the special experience of being allowed to look intimately inside the lives of hundreds of other people. This extra vantage point has helped me understand many of the basic truths necessary for emotional health. I want to pass this knowledge along to you in hopes that it may help you during your own journey through life.

In the following chapters, you will learn a variety of truths that are important for emotional health. You will be shown ways to use these truths to free yourself from the lies that are causing you needless emotional misery. To give you an idea of what this book has in store for you and just how revitalizing the truth can be, let's resume the session I had with Bill.

THERE'S ALWAYS A CHOICE

I looked down at my note pad where I'd been making some notes while Bill told me about his difficulties.

"All right, Bill, let's look at the truth of the situation with your son," I began. "Why wouldn't you let him be held back last year when his teacher suggested it?"

"Because I was stupid," said Bill. "I should have listened to the teacher and trusted her suggestion."

I shook my head. "No, you didn't make that decision because you were stupid, Bill. The truth is, you aren't stupid. So I'll ask you again: Why wouldn't you let your son be held back last year?"

Bill looked full-faced at me, blinked a few times, then stammered, "Because . . . because I hoped my son would get better without having to face the pain and embarrassment of being held back. I didn't want the other kids to make fun of him as if he were some stupid idiot. I kept hoping for some kind of a miracle where he'd wake up one morning and just start to read. I wanted to believe in him when nobody else would."

"And now, Bill? Why are you willing to let him be held back now?"

"Because it's what's best for him. I can see that now. He was in over his head and he will always be unless we can do something now to help him out. As painful as it will be for him, keeping him back a year will help him learn to read better and catch up on what he has already missed."

I nodded my head in agreement.

"You're a good father, Bill. Better than you realize. You let fatherly concern and hurt for your son get in the way of doing what was best for him at first, but you saw your mistake and corrected it. You saw the truth that the only way your son would really learn to read was through the pain of repeating the same grade. While it hurt to admit it to yourself, you faced the truth that there is no gain without pain. Seeing that truth helped free you up to do what was right for your son. But you seem to be missing an important truth that might help you out a little."

"You've got my attention. What truth am I missing?" he asked.

"One you have heard a thousand times before but seem to have quit applying to yourself, that to err is human. As trite as that truth may sound, it is one of the truths you are needing the most right now. You aren't cutting yourself much slack about what you did regarding your son or concerning what happened at work, and you are feeling like a failure as a father and a worker when you are actually pretty good at both."

Bill slowly sat back in his chair. He massaged his face with his hands, then relaxed his shoulders. I could hear a soft sigh ease out of him.

"I see what you are after. I really don't allow myself to make mistakes with my kids or at work either. I guess I have forgotten that making mistakes is pretty human."

"It's a truth that is easy to forget, but it's emotionally deadly when we do. Truths like 'To err is human' and 'There is no gain without pain' are the building blocks of emotional health in life. If we get away from them, we emotionally suffer in ways that could have been avoided. The suffering you have been experiencing isn't so much tied to your son's reading problems or the job setback or the struggles with your wife as it is tied to your having gotten away from these and other basic truths."

"That sheds a new light on things. When you mentioned that the truth sets people free, I guess I kind of lightly passed it off as one of those well-intentioned sayings that doesn't mean much. But it really is true. Heh, how about another round?"

"Sure. Let's look at that situation with your wife and the new house. You said you didn't feel as though you had any choice in that matter, that you have to buy the house whether you can afford it or not."

"Uh-huh."

"Well, what about that, Bill? Is that really the truth? Do you have to buy the house? Can your wife force you to buy that new home?"

"Well . . . not literally force . . . that is, she can't actually make me sign the . . . what I mean is . . . uh. . . ."

"What you are saying is that you do have a choice," I injected, pushing him to confront the situation squarely. "Nobody—not even your wife—can force you to do something you know is careless and illogical. Isn't that true?"

Bill's forehead furrowed in thought. He turned serious.

"Yeah," he agreed. "Well, of course I have a choice." He paused, then added, "I don't have to buy the house my wife wants. I guess I tell myself I have to and end up feeling trapped by that. Maybe I trap myself."

"I think that's right, Bill. We often tell ourselves things like, 'I have to do this' and 'I have to do that,' only to feel trapped. We end up doing things that we either don't want to do or know to be wrong to do, or both. In a very real way, we do trap ourselves with this 'have to' mind-set when the real truth is that we don't have to do anything we don't believe is right to do. You and your wife have a tough decision to make together regarding whether or not to buy a new home, but it is important for you to realize that you don't have to buy one. That truth may free you up to pursue what you feel is best rather than give in to keep her pacified and then resent the whole thing once it's done."

"This truth stuff is starting to make some sense," Bill admitted. "I didn't realize that I had gotten so far away from some basic truths about life. I can see how some of the emotional strain I have been feeling is related to having forgotten these truths. I've learned more today than I thought I would. What you've said has really helped me. Uh, maybe next time we can talk about some other things that have been bothering me. I could stand to get the truth figured out on those things too."

"I'll look forward to it," I said. "We'll work through this together."

And we did. I met with Bill once a week for the next six months. We talked a lot. I asked questions that continually pushed Bill to examine the truth related to whatever his problems were. He became very good at facing the truth without losing his sense of optimism about life. Bill's emotional health improved dramatically. At the end of this book, I will reintroduce you to Bill and give you a final look at his efforts to live a life based on truth.

PUTTING TRUTH ON YOUR SIDE

What Bill learned about truth, you can learn. You can learn to face life with truth as your compass. Just as Bill did, you can achieve emotional health by knowing and doing the truth. But first, some words of perspective.

None of the truths that I will discuss in the coming chapters are new. Solomon, the wisest man who ever lived, said there is nothing new under the sun. Time has shown he was right about this. As you read about each truth, you may find yourself thinking, *I've heard this before* or *Tell me something I don't already know.* But please don't think you really know or understand these truths just because you may have heard them before.

Truths need to be examined and discussed even if you have heard them thousands of times before. As A. P. Herbert put it, "Imagine how little good music there would be if, for example, a conductor refused to play Beethoven's 'Fifth Symphony' on the ground that his audience may have heard it before." Think about how few truths we could discuss if we couldn't discuss the ones we have already heard.

The truths discussed in this book, like a fine symphony, need to be heard over and over again until you understand every little measure of what they mean. They are *that* important. My hope is to explore these "old" truths in a way that might make them clearer, more meaningful, even life changing. Things that have been around awhile do have a way of losing their freshness and power. So it is with truths that have survived the centuries. Thus, I will try to give these familiar truths new interpretations and contemporary applications. If you are like most people, you don't need "new" truths as much as you need to take more seriously the "old" truths that you have already heard.

The next section of the book contains what I believe

to be twelve of the most important truths for an emotionally healthy life. By dedicating your life to these
truths, you can have the kind of emotional health you
have always yearned for. Read on and see what you
think. As you read about these truths, I will show you
practical ways to put them to use in your life. At the
end of each chapter you'll be given a chance to apply
what you have learned to your own daily confronta-
tions and challenges. Finally, at the end of the book I
will try to challenge your thinking about whether or
not there is an ultimate source of truth and what it
might mean for your life if there is.

PART TWO

■

THURMAN'S
TOP
TWELVE
TRUTHS
FOR AN
EMOTIONALLY
HEALTHY
LIFE

CHAPTER 2

∎

To Err Is Human

If at first you don't succeed,
you're running about average.
M. H. Alderson

You've heard it all your life, right? "To err is human, to forgive, divine." Sure, you've heard it. But I would be willing to bet you don't really *believe* that making mistakes is normal. My guess is that you go out each day trying to be perfect or semi-perfect and then feel disappointed, if not outright annoyed, whenever you make a mistake. Deep down in your private stock of hidden beliefs, you probably are still hanging on to the notion that you should earn an A+ in all areas of your life, all the time.

Most of us hate to make mistakes. And it's not just because they require the time and energy to correct. It's because they are evidence of something we don't want to face: the fact that we aren't flawless. So many of us try in vain to be flawless, all in an effort to keep stiff-arming the basic truth that we are anything but. Something about accepting the fact that we are imperfect irritates us. So we keep trying to be perfect, even though we cannot be.

Now, don't get me wrong. I'm not against the fighting spirit of "never say die" if the cause is worthy. I cheered every time Rocky Balboa got up off the mat after being knocked down. We love and admire the person who goes the distance.

I had coaches in school who drilled me with all the rah-rah cliches—"Winners never quit and quitters never win"; "When the going gets tough, the tough get going"; "No pain, no gain"—and to some extent I can endorse that. I'm not in favor of throwing in the towel the first time things don't work out.

What worries me is when the fanaticism for perfection makes us believe that making a mistake of any kind proves that we are worthless as individuals. That's not only ridiculous but dangerous.

"How," you may ask, "is it dangerous?"

A person who believes that to err is stupid will make a mistake and immediately start into a self-abusive song and dance that goes like this:

> *You stupid idiot! What's wrong with you? How could you have ever done something so imbecilic! No one else on the planet has ever done anything this ignorant. You are the only person dumb enough to have pulled this off. Great work, chump! Everyone around you must think you are the biggest moron ever born. You deserve the miserable life you're leading because you are nothing but a loser from the word go. Hang your head in shame.*

This poor person's levels of anger, anxiety, guilt, embarrassment, and worry must go sky-high with this kind of self-flagellation going on in his or her mind. Imagine the damage this must do to this person's sense of competence and value. The devastating effect it also has on this person's ability to relate to others is immeasurable. Overall, the to err is stupid notion is one of the most emotionally damaging views any of us can try to cope with.

The person who believes to err is human approaches errors and failure differently. The minute he or she makes a mistake, the internal reaction is something like this:

> *I just messed up. I don't like it, but I did. This will take some time to correct, so I'd better get started on it. This is the same thing Linda did yesterday. Now I know how she must have felt. In fact, I see people make this sort of mistake all the time. I want to make as few mistakes as possible, so I'll try to correct what led to this mistake. This isn't the end of the world. After all, I am only human.*

This person's emotional volume stays at a pretty tolerable level, a level that doesn't get in the way of correcting mistakes and moving on. This person doesn't inflict unnecessary pain on himself or herself just because of a mistake. The mistake itself was painful and costly enough. Creating further damage via emotional self-abuse makes no sense. This second person is not at odds with human frailties; he or she can face them, even accept them, and then move on. And that's emotionally healthy.

Why wasn't the first person able to think this way? Some people have extremely strong feelings of shame and inferiority deep within themselves. These feelings dominate their lives, like an anvil resting on their shoulders, weighing them down as they trudge up the stairs of life. And then, as if the heaviness of the shame and inferiority feelings weren't bad enough, they come up with a solution that only makes things worse. They convince themselves that if they can just avoid making mistakes, it will drive away the feelings of inferiority.

These to-err-is-stupid folks feel so bad about themselves they believe the only way they can conquer their problem is to go to the other extreme: They try to be perfect. Of course, this only exacerbates the problem. They can never be totally successful because each new mistake they make underscores their lack of perfection and, thus, leads to even more self-abuse and depression. The cycle is vicious and endless.

ANGER AND MISTAKES: FREQUENT BEDFELLOWS

Alicia, one of my patients, struggles on a very deep level with accepting the truth that to err is, indeed, very human. She has spent her whole life believing just the opposite and, thus, hating herself every time she makes any kind of mistake. By helping her recall her past, I learned she was severely criticized as a child whenever she made a mistake. She was indoctrinated by her parents to believe that personal errors were intolerable. Now, as an adult, she has continued to follow that early path.

Problems with anger and depression caused Alicia to seek counseling, but she often used our sessions to defend her belief that mistakes were the norm for everyone but her. I challenged her on this as often as I could, hoping to knock down the wall she had erected to hide her humanity. Here is an example of how one of our typical sessions went:

"What would you like to talk about today?" I asked.

"Well, I've been feeling really angry this week. Toward everything. The littlest thing can set me off," said Alicia.

"Tell me more."

"Some things at work haven't been going well. I messed up a letter I was supposed to do for my boss. That was really stupid. Then, when I got home, I yelled at Chuck for not doing something he said he would do for me."

"What do you think is causing your anger?" I prodded.

"I don't know. You're the doctor, you tell me," Alicia answered half-jokingly, not really wanting to look at herself.

"Come on, Alicia, give it a try. I think you know what's going on, don't you?"

"You want me to admit that I don't want myself or anyone else around me to make mistakes and that when I do, or they do, my anger explodes. That's what you want me to say, right?"

I shook my head. "What *I* want you to say isn't important. The point is, what's the truth? Isn't that what we're really after in these sessions?"

"I guess so," she said, reluctantly, "but it seems to me that making mistakes is really stupid and completely avoidable. I just can't stand it when stupid things like that happen."

I looked directly at Alicia. "I think we both know these ideas about mistakes being stupid were trained into you a long time ago."

Alicia rolled her eyes upward. "All roads lead home, eh?" she ventured. "All right, yes, I got it from my parents. They never let up on me. They were constantly on my case. I could never measure up to their yardstick, and they would beat me with it when I didn't."

Suddenly, bitter tears formed in her eyes.

"The way they treated you hurt a lot, didn't it?" I responded, hoping to keep the tears flowing. She needed the emotional relief.

"Yes. A lot," Alicia replied.

"It seems to me that your parents used a standard that no one could have measured up to, but you've never realized that. You've continued to use that same yardstick ever since then."

"I guess I have. I certainly never seem to measure up, and, for that matter, no one else seems to be measuring up to my yardstick either," she admitted.

"Well, I'll tell you what I think. When no one measures up, it's time to change the yardstick."

"Could be," she answered, not really sounding committed to the idea.

"Alicia, I believe that *if* you're willing to take a truthful look at the yardstick you were handed by your parents—the one you've been using ever since you left them—you'll see that you need to throw it away and replace it with a more realistic and humane one. Your parents taught you that to err was stupid, inexcusable, and unforgivable. Like all other children, you believed your parents. Unfortunately, in this area, they were wrong. You need to recognize that. You'll never get over your chronic struggles with anger and depression until you allow yourself to make a few mistakes. Even some big ones."

"I will never accept the idea that making mistakes

is all right," she defiantly replied, replaying the mental tape her parents had put inside her.

"Then you will never get better!" I said, just as defiantly.

"You're telling me I have to *like* my mistakes?"

"No," I replied. "Accepting mistakes and liking them are two different things. I'm just telling you honestly that if you keep refusing to accept the fact that making mistakes is part of life—yours and everybody else's—you won't ever become emotionally healthy. You certainly don't have to like your mistakes, but you need to see them as part of being human."

"Sounds like an awfully fine line between accepting and liking."

"Maybe. But it's one worth distinguishing."

Alicia shrugged. "I'll tell you straight out, I don't really want to do what you say. Still, I know I need to do something. I'll give it a try and see how it goes."

"That's a start," I encouraged her. "I'm confident you can pull this off."

HOW HUMAN IS MAKING MISTAKES?

Is making mistakes human or not? Your decision about this, like Alicia's was, will be crucially important. If you decide that mistakes are aberrations, you'll be in for a lifetime of self-abuse and emotional misery. If, on the other hand, you can see the truth that mistakes are an inescapable reality of being a fallible human being, you will experience a lifetime of growth and peace.

Now again, let me emphasize that "To err is human" does not mean we have a license to make mistakes all over the place or not to try to correct our mistakes. You can't expect to succeed in life if you have the attitude, "Well, since I can't be perfect, I'll just be imperfect but not worry about it." A lack of genuine concern for quality is just as grievous a mistake as the desire to be perfect. Both are failures to deal with the truth. We are imperfect, but we are capable of quality and improvement.

Yes, we'll all make mistakes. But making them out of indifference or carelessness isn't healthy. As Jerry Jenkins humorously put it, "To err is human, but when the eraser wears out ahead of your pencil, you're overdoing it."

HOW TO DISCERN TRUTH

What ultimately helped Alicia come to grips with her obsession with perfection was a helpful exercise that can be just as beneficial to you.

The exercise involves using what I call the TRUTH system.[1] Each letter in the acronym TRUTH stands for an important issue in your effort to achieve emotional maturity. Let me explain them.

The first *T* stands for "trigger event." This is an event or situation that happens to you. For example, you might be at a movie and someone behind you might start talking too loud. Or you might be rushing to get to an appointment and accidentally lock your keys in your car. Or, on a more serious level, you might be fired from your job or perhaps informed of the sudden, unexpected death of a loved one.

The *R* stands for "reflection." This is the time you spend thinking about what has just happened and is often referred to as "self-talk." If you found your keys were locked inside the car, you might think some-thing like, *What a stupid idiot I am. What kind of moron locks his keys in his car at a time like this? Incredible! Now I'll miss my appointment and everybody will end up mad at me. What a jerk I am!*

The *U* stands for "unhealthy response." These are the unhealthy physiological, emotional, and behav-ioral reactions to the trigger event and your reflec-tions about it that manifest themselves. These are un-necessarily painful and unproductive. For example, when you become overly frustrated and angry about the car keys, your physiological reaction will proba-bly be an increased heart rate, muscle tension, and shortness of breath. Your emotional reaction might be a combination of heightened anger and anxiety. Your behavioral reaction might be that you kick the car door and pound on the hood. All these reactions not only hurt you but don't get your keys out of the car.

The second *T* stands for "truth." At this point you need to make yourself face the truth about the trigger event. For example, in this chapter we learned that to err is human. So, as you stand outside your car, you might say, "Okay, this is inconvenient, but lots of people make the same mistake every day. I'm not the first guy to lock his keys in his car. This doesn't make me an idiot. I'm not happy about it, but then again, it's not the end of the world. If people get mad at me for being late, I'll tell them exactly what happened. No doubt they've done the same thing." The primary emphasis here is on telling yourself as much truth as you possibly can in order to fight the lies and distor-tions you told yourself back at the "reflection" stage.

And, finally, the *H* stands for "healthy response." After telling yourself the truth, you should find yourself reacting in an emotionally healthier manner than you did during the "reflection" stage. For example, after telling yourself the truth about locking your keys in your car, you may find yourself being calmer, less angry, and moving in the direction of finding some help so that you can resolve your dilemma.

Now, initially, you may tell yourself the truth and find that you don't feel or behave differently. In other words, sometimes we tell ourselves the truth and remain just as upset as we were to begin with. For my patient Alicia, this was a common situation at first. Don't get discouraged, however. This only means that the faulty and erroneous thoughts you had during the "reflection" stage were extremely deep and well-rehearsed. It will take some time and work before you will be able to replace such self-destructive thoughts —such lies—with the truth.

NOW YOU GIVE IT A TRY

You learned two important things in this chapter: first, that to err really is human; second, that you can use the TRUTH system to help you cope with any of life's challenges or crises. All right, let's now combine the two. I am going to present you with a scenario and you can put the TRUTH system into use to prove (for the betterment of your emotional health) that to err is human. Use the space provided to journal as you think about your responses.

Let's say that you are at a very important social event and you are dressed in an expensive outfit. Suddenly, without warning, a greasy, red-sauced hors d'oeuvre slips off the toothpick you are holding and spills down the front of your blouse or shirt. That is the "trigger event" that will set everything in motion.

Now, what do you think you would say to yourself if this happened to you? Write down what you think your thoughts would be.

_____

_____

_____

What physiological reactions do you think you would have?

_____

_____

_____

What emotions would you feel if this happened to you?

_____

_____

_____

Finally, how would you have reacted behaviorally?

_____

_____

_____

I would have reacted something like this:

Trigger Event: spilled an hors d'oeuvre on my nice, clean shirt.

Reflection: *Thurman, you stupid idiot. Only a socially ungracious slug like you would do something as stupid as this. No one else at this party did something this stupid. You look like a clown with no circus to go to. Every eye in the place is on you. You will be lucky if you ever get invited to another social event the rest of your life.*

Unhealthy Responses:
Physiological—heart starts to race, muscles tense up, begin to sweat.
Emotional—feel anxious, humiliated, embarrassed, uncomfortable.
Behavioral—immediately cover up the spot on my shirt with my hand and hurriedly walk to the rest-room where I feverishly work on getting out the stain.

Now, it is time for *T*—the Truth—to show up and help us out. In this scenario, what is the truth about what happened? Take a minute to write down what the truth is about spilling something on yourself at an important social event.

_____

_____

_____

_____

Well, how did you do with facing the truth? How many truths were you able to come up with concerning the event? You may not have been able to come up with any or you may have come up with several. Perhaps you were somewhere in between. One thing is certain, however: You're seeing that it is a challenge to find and face the truth.

For me, the truth in this situation might be something like this:

Hey, you just made a mistake. It isn't the end of the world. Nobody really noticed, and, even if they did, they probably felt some empathy pains for you. Maybe you can even make a joke out of it to put everyone at ease (tell the host and hostess that not only did you enjoy the hors d'oeuvres but your shirt did too). Be thankful it wasn't battery acid you spilled on your shirt. Now, go clean yourself up and get back to enjoying the party.

How do you think your *H* phase ("healthy response") would have turned out? Imagine how you would feel after telling yourself the truth. Would the *T* ("truth") really have helped you calm down physiologically, emotionally, or behaviorally, or would you have remained quite upset about the whole thing?

If the truth would not have calmed you down, you might want to take a minute now and consider why. Maybe you, like Alicia first did, have gotten to a point where the truth isn't as powerful or strong as it needs to be to help you out. Maybe your mental truth "muscle" has atrophied through lack of exercise over the years. Be of good cheer. <u>With practice, the truth can become stronger than anything else in your thoughts.</u> Working out the truth can and will lead you to the emotional health you have been wanting.

Don't worry if you have trouble figuring out each part of the TRUTH system at first. It will be like riding a bike. You may feel a bit awkward, but it will become second nature with time and practice. To make sure you keep practicing the truth, I will review the TRUTH system with you at the end of the coming chapters.

CHAPTER 3

■

What "Should" Have Happened Did

For my part, whatever anguish of spirit it may cost, I am willing to know the whole truth; to know the worst, and to provide for it.

—Patrick Henry

L isten to people talk and you will often hear them use the word *should* or some variation of it:

"I shouldn't have said that."

"Jeff should have been on time."

"My parents shouldn't have treated me that way when I was younger."

"Ann should have let me know about that yesterday."

"Things should be different from the way they are."

Whenever I hear (or use) the word *should*, a red flag goes up in my mind that warns me that reality just got stiff-armed. What do I mean? Well, think about it for a minute. *Should* is most often used in reference to some sort of ideal setting in a perfect world.

Using *should* is our way of saying we don't like the reality we face. To say, "He shouldn't have been so late" actually means, "I can't accept the fact that he was so late." It means that we have a vision of some perfect world in which people are never late and we can't stand it when someone violates that world. Using the word *should* represents an unwillingness on our part to deal with reality as it is.

The reality is that if someone isn't being careful about the time, how could he be anything but late? Can a person who doesn't manage his time well and waits too long before leaving get somewhere on time? In a word, no. What I'm suggesting here is that it really doesn't make sense to say something like, "He shouldn't have been late," when everything the person did worked toward making sure he would be late.

One person who seemed to understand the real meaning of the word *should* was the late University of Alabama head football coach Paul "Bear" Bryant. The Crimson Tide football team was heavily favored to win a game against an inferior opponent. Instead, Alabama lost. During the post-game interview, Coach Bryant was asked, "How do you feel about losing a game you *should* have won?" His reported reply was, "What should have happened did."

What Coach Bryant was saying was, "Look, guys, throw out all of that 'the better team always wins' stuff. We fumbled the ball, threw interceptions, and missed a lot of blocks. The other team didn't. Given that we played badly and they played well, the game turned out just as it *should* have."

I'd say Coach Bryant had a pretty good understanding of reality and a willingness to deal with it rather than avoid it.

Whenever I am attempting to help a patient work through some painful reality in his or her life, I know we have a lot of work to do if that person says, "I shouldn't have done what I did" or "They shouldn't have acted that way toward me." These kinds of statements tell me the patient hasn't accepted reality. Until the truth of a situation is accepted *as it is*, it's impossible to be genuinely emotionally healthy. Let me give you a specific example from one of my counseling sessions.

Cheryl was an unhappy woman. She was attractive, she was married to a fine man, and she had three terrific young children. But Cheryl also had serious emotional problems. She came to see me to help her deal with a chronic struggle she had with depression and low self-esteem. As we explored her childhood, she revealed that she had been sexually abused by her father. This was tremendously painful for her, as you might well imagine, and she had an extremely difficult time coming to grips with the fact that it really had happened.

Discussing the sexual abuse during one of our sessions, Cheryl tearfully blurted out, "He shouldn't have done what he did to me." In that one statement, I knew that Cheryl had not yet faced what had happened to her. Instead, she was still holding on to a more idealized view of father-daughter relationships and, even more broadly, of the world at large. To challenge her thinking on the matter, I asked her a question that took her by surprise.

"Why shouldn't he have done what he did?"

"What do you mean?" Cheryl demanded, almost screaming at me. "Are you saying it was okay for him to sexually abuse me?"

"No, of course not. But you said he *shouldn't* have abused you, as if fathers never do that sort of thing."

"Well, they *shouldn't* do that kind of thing," she shot back.

"Cheryl, I hear you saying you wish he hadn't abused you, and I certainly wish he hadn't too. What he did was horrible. But in the real world some fathers *do* sexually abuse their daughters. Your father was a very disturbed man, and disturbed men sometimes abuse their daughters. It isn't right, and I am *not* asking you to say you are glad he did; but saying he shouldn't have done what he did isn't seeing the situation as it really was. His sexual abuse of you was consistent with how sick a man he was. In fact, given how disturbed a person he was, it would have been *more* surprising if he *hadn't* sexually abused you."

Cheryl became furious. "What am I supposed to say then," she retorted bitterly, "that I feel so much better now that I know he was consistent with the level of sickness he had?"

"Not at all," I assured her. "I'm simply trying to help you see that by saying he shouldn't have sexually abused you, you are refusing to deal with the fact that he did. You're continuing to hide from the truth of what he did and how much that still hurts you. If you keep saying, 'He shouldn't have,' you are going to keep running from the painful fact that he did. If you won't face what he did to you, you won't be able to heal the wounds he gave you. You do want to get better, don't you?"

"Yes, yes." Cheryl wrung her hands. "I *have* to get over this. It has scarred my life. But I just can't accept what he did. No father should do that to his daughter."

Again she was saying the word *should*.

"And no father in his *right mind* does that to his daughter," I countered. "That's not the act of a healthy, loving father toward his daughter. But you, Cheryl, had a very unhealthy and unloving father who used you to act out his sickness. I wish he hadn't hurt you. But I want you to face the fact that he did. You can't face it by saying he *shouldn't* have done it."

THE DELUSION OF *SHOULD*

You may be identifying with Cheryl, at least on the level of how often you hide behind the delusion of how you feel things should be as opposed to accepting the reality of how you know they are.

I know that I can identify with Cheryl. I often find myself saying things like, "Now, I shouldn't have done that" or "Life just shouldn't be that way." In my own way, I find myself mentally living in some perfect world that doesn't exist so that I can run from the sometimes painful *real* world that *does* exist. I can see the damage these *shoulds* do to my own emotional health.

My weekly workouts at the racquetball court come to mind as an example. I frequently catch myself saying, "Shoot, I shouldn't have missed that." But that's not true. Given the fact that I wasn't watching the ball very closely and that I didn't get my racquet back quickly enough to hit it properly, *what should have happened did.* I missed.

Hey, that's what happens if you don't pay attention to what you're doing. And until I accept the fact that missing that shot is what *should* have happened, I will never start to work on improving my concentration. I won't improve. I won't get better. I'll just sit there belittling myself, focusing on the past (the missed shot), and more than likely I will continue to miss other shots in the future.

The same goes for you. The next time you are tempted to say the word *should*, pause first to apply the truth of "what should have happened did" to it. If you miss an appointment because you forgot it, don't say, "I *should* have remembered." No, you forgot the appointment because you, as a human being, don't always remember everything you commit to do and sometimes things get pushed to the back of your memory. "I should have remembered the appointment" really means "I can't accept the fact that I forgot the appointment." Until you accept the fact that you forgot it, you won't correct whatever it was that led you to forget it.

FINDING THE TRUTH HIDDEN BEHIND YOUR *SHOULDS*

I'm pleased to say that my patient Cheryl learned how to see the truth behind her use of the word *should.* She eventually realized that she too often was refusing to deal not only with what her father had done to her but also with other painful issues in her life by simply saying, "That *shouldn't* have happened" or "This shouldn't be." I helped her see how this mind-set was keeping her in the past, focusing on what *had* happened to her rather than on what now *could* be going on in her life to overcome it. She committed herself to spending less time in the ideal world of what "should be" and more time in the real world dealing with *what is.*

I also showed Cheryl that the word *should* often shows up in our interactions with other people too. We all need to be alert to this. If, for example, your older son shoves your younger daughter, it isn't realistic to say to the son, "You shouldn't have done that!" There are two reasons: first, he has already done it and simply saying he shouldn't have done it won't change the fact that he did; and second, given the fact that your son is young, immature, and a rough-and-tumble boy, what he did was pretty consistent with who he is. Of course, behavior that is consistent with one's instinctive nature or personality is not necessarily acceptable. So, in this instance, the correct action is to tell him that you do not want him to shove his sister again *and* if he does he will be disciplined. You are now dealing with his misbehavior in the here and now rather than rubbing his nose in the there and then.

MAINTAINING YOUR MOMENTUM

As we ended chapter 2 you were taught the TRUTH system. You had a chance to apply it specifically to the statement, "To err is human." I promised you I would give you more opportunities to put that TRUTH system into action.

Now, here's how we are going to go about it. For a complete week, I want you to chronicle the things that "trigger" your emotional problems in life. I want you to write them in a TRUTH journal.

If you make a mistake (like lock your keys in your car) or encounter some unpleasant life situation (like a long line at the grocery store) consider these your *T* factors ("trigger events"). Write them down in your journal.

Recall next what lies you told yourself at that moment (or what lies you have been telling yourself over and over for many years about this situation). This will be the *R* stage ("reflection"). Write these lies in your journal. If you need some help figuring out what the lies are that you tell yourself, you can read my previous book *The Lies We Believe* (Nashville: Thomas Nelson, 1989).

Next, note how you reacted physically, emotionally, and behaviorally to the circumstances. This will be the *U* phase ("unhealthy response"). Be specific in your journal about your pulse rate, breathing, feelings of nervousness or anxiety or anger or depression, and behavioral reactions to the event.

After that, write down very rationally and logically what truths you told *or needed to tell* yourself about that situation. This will be the second *T* phase ("truth"). If your mind goes blank and you can't come up with any truth, be honest in noting that. If you come up with a truthful statement, but on later reflection, it really doesn't seem appropriate to that circumstance, note it anyway. Keeping this journal is a discovery exercise.

Finally, record in your journal how recalling these truths helped you handle the situation in a healthier manner. This will be the summary or *H* conclusion to the procedure ("healthy response"). As we proceed with other chapters you may want to continue to use your journal to monitor how much progress you are making with the truth.

CHAPTER 4

■

You Can't Please Everyone

> I cannot give you the formula for success, but I can give you the formula for failure—try to please everybody.
>
> —Herbert Bayard Swope

In 1975 singer Rick Nelson recorded a song I really liked called "Garden Party." In the song, Rick Nelson told of being invited to sing in an "oldies" concert at Madison Square Garden. When he got on stage, he sang several of his newest songs and the crowd booed and hissed at him. That wasn't what they had paid to hear. They wanted him to do "Hello, Mary Lou" and "Traveling Man" and his other hit singles from the 1950s and 1960s. In the song "Garden Party," Rick Nelson surmised, "You can't please everyone, so you've got to please yourself."

Whereas I am not so sure about the "so you've got to please yourself" part of that phrase (it sounds a little bit too self-centered for my tastes), I do think the "you can't please everyone" line is one of the great truths we need to recognize and practice in order to lead emotionally strong lives. To some extent Rick Nelson must have come to this realization, for the last line in his song was, "If memories were all I sang, I'd rather drive a truck."

Yes, I know—"You can't please everyone" is a one-liner you've already heard a million times. But hearing it and believing it are not always the same thing. Most people (yes, including you) are out there every day trying to please most everyone. Consider how much you worry about whether or not people like you and if they are happy with what you do. Why does it put a knot in your stomach whenever someone is upset with you? Why are you willing to do almost *anything* to insure that people will be pleased with you?

The answer is that we all have a basic need of approval. We want people to tell us we are all right, acceptable, special, worthy of love and admiration and trust and respect. In fact, if we *don't* receive adequate approval from people, we find it hard to get through life. A problem arises, however, when we think we need to earn the admiration and approval of every human being we meet. That simply is impossible and we can emotionally wipe ourselves out proving it.

The origins of this neurotic need to please everyone, and thereby gain their approval, often go back to childhood where there was a real (or perhaps perceived) lack of love and approval from one or both parents. This missing element of personal development created an internal vacuum for love that remained very hard to fill. Later, in adult life, it became virtually impossible for one person (a spouse or good friend) to meet all the approval needs of the deprived person.

Jim, one of my patients who came to see me because of marital problems, struggled with an extremely strong need to please everyone and to receive everyone's approval. During his childhood, Jim had been ignored by his father. Jim's father hadn't criticized him or hit him or yelled at him. He had just ignored him. He was so caught up in his career, he never had time to play catch with Jim or read a book together or go camping or just sit around the television with popcorn. Jim interpreted this as rejection.

Feeling rejected by the most important male in his life, Jim spent the rest of his life trying to make up for this missing love by doing his best to make everyone else like him, especially his boss, his colleagues, and his clients.

"My wife and I had another one of those heated arguments the other day," Jim told me at the start of one of our sessions.

"What caused it?" I asked.

"Same as always. She thinks I work too much. I'm usually the last guy out of the office every night. That puts me home late. And even then, I have a briefcase filled with contracts to review, proposals to analyze, and ad campaigns to design. My wife says she is so far down on my list of priorities, we might as well not even be married."

"What do you think about that?"

Jim shrugged his shoulders. "Well, I guess if actions speak louder than words, she's probably right. She just doesn't understand, though, that I have a lot of responsibilities and a lot of people who are depending on me."

One glance at Jim showed that he was physically exhausted. There were bags under his eyes, a pallor to his skin, and his posture was slumped and heavy.

"Sounds like your workaholism is jeopardizing your relationship with your wife and ruining your health, Jim," I told him flatly. "Why do you think you continually get yourself involved in so many different things?"

Jim's eyes avoided mine. "I don't know."

"Do you remember our discussion about how you felt about never receiving any approval from your father?"

"Yes, sure, I remember."

"And do you remember how you decided that because of that you developed a heightened need to have people like you and approve of you? You admitted back then that you were deathly afraid of ever making anyone displeased with you."

"Yes, I know," he said.

"Well, then, let me ask you this: Do you see any connection between the flurry of activities you are now caught up in and the hurt you felt from being ignored by your dad?"

"That happened thirty years ago," said Jim, ducking the question. "What does that have to do with my life now?"

"I think you know," I insisted. "You do know, don't you?"

"This is where I'm supposed to say that I'm still looking for my father's approval by doing all these other things," he said with a false tone of indifference. "You expect me to say that since I couldn't please my old man, I'm now trying to please everybody else I come in contact with. It's my unfulfilled need to find love and approval, right?"

"That's it exactly," I agreed. "We both know that. But don't you see the irony in all this? In seeking something to substitute for the approval and love your father never gave you, you've been going 'all out' for your boss, your co-workers, your customers and everybody—everybody except your wife. And *she's* the one who wants to give you all the love and approval a man could ever want. You're treating her exactly the way your father treated you."

This seemed to strike a chord in Jim. He sat silently for nearly a minute weighing what I'd said. Finally, he spoke.

"The last person in the world I'd want as a role model would be my father. Heaven forbid, I should ever become a carbon copy of him. It's just that . . . well, I've gone so many years trying to get people to like me, I don't know if I can change. I know that if I pulled back on some of these projects I'm tied to, I'd upset a lot of folks. Some of the men, especially, would really be angry with me. That worries me."

"But listen to yourself, Jim," I insisted. "You're saying that at the expense of your personal health and the security of your marriage, you're still more concerned with trying to please everyone. Isn't that a rather high price to pay?"

Again, Jim paused. "What's . . . what's wrong with me, Dr. Thurman? When I hear you outline my life for me, I see how ridiculous it is to be living like this. But then, I just go out and continue to live that way. Why am I behaving like this?"

"Have you ever considered that your compulsion to please everyone may be an addiction, Jim?"

Jim's eyes widened. "An *addiction!* I would never have thought of it in terms like that. But . . . well, it kind of makes sense, doesn't it? I'm like a drug addict. If I can get a regular dose of approval, then I'm fine. But if I go any place where there might not be anyone to pat me on the back or pay me a compliment, it's like I go into withdrawal. I can't handle that. I need a 'fix' of approval on a regular basis. It's frightening to think of it like that. I'm hooked on my need for approval. I've got to do something about this."

"How would you handle it if you were addicted to drugs?" I asked him.

"I'd . . . well, I'd quit," he stammered. "I'd stop taking that poison. I'd clean out my system. I'd purge myself of the addiction."

"It would be painful," I reminded him. "It hurts to go through withdrawal from *any* kind of addiction."

"But that would be a matter of life and death," Jim responded, a sense of genuine anxiety coming over him.

"So is your addiction to approval," I warned him. "The way you look right now, it's obvious you're headed for serious problems."

"You're right," Jim said seriously. "I'm hooked on approval and I need to break the habit. Until today, I didn't want to see that."

A CURE FOR THE ADDICTION

Were there parts of Jim's confession you could relate to? Although the truth is that we *can't* please everyone all the time, a lot of people seem to keep trying anyway. If you find yourself seeking everyone's approval, don't deceive yourself into thinking it is not an addiction. It is.

For too many people, approval is the "drug" they crave night and day. But like any comparable street drug, the effects of approval are short-lived and the addict all too quickly needs to "score" again so he or she can shoot up once more. It's a vicious cycle, dangerous and life-threatening, but preventable.

If you consider yourself to be a person who craves continuous approval, take some positive steps to "go straight." Begin by admitting you have the addiction. Don't delay facing up to it or hiding it. Next, think of all the people you have around you who will accept you *as you are.* Be appreciative of a loving spouse, a longtime college friend or buddy from the service, the close friends you have in your neighborhood and at church, and the members of your extended family. These people genuinely care for you; they aren't faithful to you just because you can do something for them.

Make an effort to cultivate some new interests which will help you meet people who will enjoy you for your company. Join a community service group, take an evening course at the local community college, become part of the church choir. You will find more than a few people at these functions who will like you for who you are, not what you do.

Emotionally healthy people often walk a sort of tightrope. They need to do a certain amount of things in order to receive a needed amount of approval from other folks. However, they realize they also need to try to please themselves in certain areas. Where Rick Nelson made his mistake at Madison Square Garden, to my way of thinking, was that he didn't divide his performance between the new songs he wanted to share with the audience and the older songs they wanted to hear.

My own life needs that same balance of give and

take. Around my home, I sometimes need to do things that my wife, Holly, wants to do or my kids want to do, even if there are other things I am more interested in doing. There are other times when I want to sit alone and read the paper or go off to the racquetball club for an afternoon simply because these things please me. Life requires balance.

My patient Jim was able to make a very positive change in his life. He was nervous about implementing some of the necessary alterations in his life, but the sincere desire to break his addiction motivated him.

I helped Jim create a list of priorities for his life. Right at the top he listed the love and care of his wife. Second, he included his need for adequate sleep, proper food, enjoyable exercise, and times of recreation. Third, he focused on his desire to do an excellent job for his employer but to stay within the confines of *his* job description rather than be an errand boy for everyone else. By adhering to these priorities, Jim took a great deal of pressure out of his life. And to his great surprise, he wound up receiving a deeper level of appreciation and approval from people than he ever would have imagined possible. Life is sometimes that way: The less you seek, the more you find.

Yet Jim also ran into disapproval from some coworkers for making decisions to remain true to his priorities. Some of his coworkers, being overly committed to work and pleasing the higher-ups, didn't like Jim's not working as hard as they were. They didn't like seeing him go home at 5 P.M. while they worked until 7 P.M. or 8 P.M. They resented Jim's taking breaks during the day while they worked through their own allotted breaks. They felt Jim should plug away at work on the weekends just as they oftentimes did.

Misery loves company, and these coworkers, probably without really being aware of it, wanted Jim to be as miserable as they were. In a very real sense, they resented his choices to be healthy as they chose to remain sick.

DOING THE TRUTH

If you, too, have led a life like Jim's, I want to challenge you to do something right now to start shaking your addiction. If you feel that you have to have everyone's approval, I want you to do something that purposely proves you can survive without it. Go yell out the time in the middle of a large store. Walk down the street wearing Mickey Mouse ears. Express a different opinion in a conversation at work tomorrow. If someone asks you to do something that you feel is an unfair request, say no.

I am not encouraging you to do anything unkind, immoral, or dangerous. I am just encouraging you to act in a manner that is consistent with the truth "You can't please everyone."

Oh, and don't be surprised that life will go on, because it will.

CHAPTER 5

■

You Don't Have To

People are always blaming their circumstances for what they are. I don't believe in circumstances.
—George Bernard Shaw

You don't have to be a cannibal to be fed up with people. You don't have to be Dutch to be somebody's Dutch uncle. You don't have to live in the south to be a Southern Baptist. You don't have to be skinny in order to go skinny dipping.

The fact is, there are a lot of things in life you don't have to be *or* do in order to be a healthy and happy individual. In fact, the less you feel you *have to* do things, the healthier and happier you will be. That may be hard for you to believe at first, especially if you have led a life in which almost everything you do feels like it has a "have to" behind it.

You'll learn in this chapter, however, just as my patient Bill (whom we discussed in chapter 1) did, that you do *not* have to buy a home you cannot afford, you do *not* have to agree with what other people tell you, and you do *not* have to feel chronically guilty over past mistakes you have made. Quite frankly, you do not have to do *anything* unless you choose to.

Have you ever noticed how often people say the

words *have to?* Have you ever noticed how often you say them? Read the trigger events and responses you recorded in your TRUTH journal in chapter 3. Are there any "have to" statements? Here are some frequently used "have to" statements. Do any of these sound familiar?

"I have to go to work tomorrow."
"I have to pay my taxes."
"I have to obey the speed limit."
"I have to go visit my parents."
"I have to finish college."
"I have to take my kids to the park Saturday."
"I have to lose some weight."

I'm sure you've said most or all of these statements at one time or another. But here is the truth: You don't *have* to go to work tomorrow. You don't *have* to pay your taxes. You don't *have* to obey the speed limit. You don't *have* to visit your parents. You don't *have* to finish college. You don't *have* to take your kids to the park on Saturday. You don't *have* to lose weight. You don't *have* to do anything if you don't want to. That's how free you are.

But there is a not-so-small hitch. You don't have to do anything, but painful consequences may come your way if you choose not to do certain things. For example, you don't have to go to work tomorrow, but you may get in trouble with your boss or possibly be fired if you don't. You don't have to pay your taxes, but you may find yourself in trouble with the IRS if you don't (they have a way of wanting to hear from you each year). You don't have to obey the speed limit, but you may get a ticket if you don't.

I think you see the *quid pro quo* going on here, right? It's very much like a law of physics: For every action there is a reaction. For every cause, there is an effect.

Now, why all the fuss about the words *have to*. Well, much like the word *should* discussed earlier, the use of the words *have to* suggests you have lost sight of the truth that what we do is done out of free choice. Allow me to point out the huge difference between a "have to" attitude toward life and a "choose to" attitude toward life.

Alan came to see me about the tremendous bitterness he felt concerning how he "had to" get married. He and his wife, Sandra, had dated off and on throughout college. Toward the end of their senior year, Sandra became pregnant with their child. As much as Alan loved Sandra, he did not feel ready for marriage. Yet he married her anyway, carrying into the marriage busloads of anger and resentment toward Sandra. During one of our sessions, Alan expressed how he felt.

"I don't know if I can ever get over this," Alan stated bluntly.

"The way you and Sandra got married bothers you a lot," I replied, trying to narrow the focus of his anger.

"I *had to* marry her," Alan replied as if the need to discuss that issue was over. "I had no choice."

"Objectively speaking, that isn't really true, is it?" I asked.

"What do you mean?" he shot back. "I'm not the kind of person to ask a girl to have a baby out of wedlock, much less go get an abortion."

"Nevertheless, those were some choices you could have made, weren't they?" I pressed.

"No, I couldn't have asked her to do those things. They were not options for me," Alan stubbornly retorted.

"Alan, you keep saying that these options weren't really options. Yet they were. You just chose not to take them," I replied just as stubbornly.

"Dr. Thurman, they were not options for me. There is no way I would have asked Sandra to have our baby out of wedlock or to abort the baby!" He refused to budge an inch and his eyes seemed to dare me to continue my line of conversation.

"Look, Alan, I think I know where your bitterness and resentment are coming from, but I'm not sure you are open to seeing it," I said gently, hoping he would let me open the door to truth just a crack.

His rigid posture relaxed slightly.

"I'm here for your help," he said at last. "I'll try to listen to what you have to say."

I smiled reassuringly and then chose my words carefully.

"It seems to me that the bitterness you're carrying around about the way you got married has to do with your refusal to see that you did have some choices, both before Sandra became pregnant and afterward," I suggested. "Prior to Sandra's becoming pregnant, you both made the choice to be sexually involved. In this day and age, being sexually involved premaritally isn't uncommon, but it was still a choice. You and she also chose not to make certain she couldn't get pregnant by not being careful about birth control.

"When she became pregnant, you both had some choices even then. Because of your personal values and feelings about abortion and adoption, you chose to get married, something you did not have to do. You and Sandra both had choices. By not being willing to admit this and take responsibility for the choices you made, you now believe that you were forced into marrying Sandra. And because you believe that you had to marry her, you resent her. You blame her and you blame the circumstances you found yourself in for why you got married rather than take responsibility for the personal choices you made all along the way that helped create those circumstances."

Alan started to squirm in his chair. I could tell that he wanted to be open-minded, but his rigid notions about his situation were still too deeply ingrained in him.

"I just can't buy that! What would you have done if you were in my shoes? Would you have felt like you had a choice?"

(It is times like this where most of us therapist types feel like pulling our hair out and going into a different line of work.)

"To be honest, Alan, probably not. But that just means I would be missing the truth too. The truth is, you had some options open to you, even if they didn't seem like options. You made the choice that best fit your values and personality. Your wife didn't make you marry her. The circumstances didn't make you marry her. You *chose* to marry her." I said this last statement with purposeful emphasis. I wanted to make it stick.

"If that is true, how is it supposed to help me with the bitterness I feel about the whole thing?"

"If you accept personal responsibility for choosing to marry Sandra, your bitterness toward her will ultimately make no sense. What would there be to be bitter about?"

"Well, I would still be bitter that I had to . . ." His voice trailed off as he realized what he was about to say again.

"I think I see what you're after," he said, "but I feel light years away from *really* believing that I didn't have to get married."

"I know that is how you feel," I said, "but becoming emotionally healthy is tied more to deeply believing the truth than to how you feel about it. The truth is, you chose to marry Sandra even though you didn't have to. She is not to blame for your choice. She owes you nothing for the decision you made. Your feelings of resentment are real, but you don't actually have a legitimate reason for being bitter toward her. These truths need to become a lot more important than how you feel right now."

TAKING RESPONSIBILITY

One of the most difficult tasks we face in life is that of taking responsibility for how we feel and what we do. The natural human bent seems to be in the direction of blaming other people or things for the unhappiness we feel and the actions we take. Yet blaming something outside of us is the ultimate cop-out.

This was the struggle underlying Alan's bitterness over his marriage to Sandra. Alan did not want to take responsibility for the choice he had made, so he fell into a "have to" mind-set that made it easy to blame Sandra for his own choice. Once he had convinced himself that he had to marry Sandra, he was able to build up a mountain of anger and bitterness toward her, as if she were the enemy. This only added more problems to his real problem.

Failure to take responsibility often underlies the emotional struggles of my patients. In both small, barely noticeable ways and big, glaring ways my patients often fail to accept responsibility for the decisions they have made in life and for the feelings those decisions help create. Helping patients take responsibility for both is one of the main tasks of counseling.

The unwillingness to accept responsibility, once recognized, is one of the main reasons therapy sometimes doesn't "work." A patient comes in with a problem he doesn't feel responsible for because he thinks it is someone else's fault. He then expects the counselor to solve this problem for him. When the counselor doesn't (because he can't), the patient often gets angry and stops coming to therapy, blaming the counselor for his lack of progress. This is a more common scenario in counseling than most people realize.

Patients who leave therapy this way often tell people, "Well, I did everything I could to deal with the problem, and nothing helped!" when he didn't really do anything of substance to face the problem responsibly. It is a real battle in counseling at times to get a patient to take responsibility for finding solutions to his problems, and the beginning point for this is helping him see that it is *his* problem.

This, then, brings us back to Alan. The truth was, he did not "have to" marry Sandra. He did have other options, even if he didn't like them. But he found it easier to blame Sandra than to see his own problem.

SEEING OPTIONS, ACCEPTING RESPONSIBILITY

In counseling Alan, I focused on helping him recognize that he did have options in the situation he faced with Sandra and that he was responsible for the decision he made.

"It's hard for me to see how I could have opted for anything but marriage to Sandra once she found out she was pregnant," Alan insisted.

"Let's try another tack, then," I suggested. "Do you have to pay taxes?"

"Yes," he said. "It's the law."

"Just because it's the law doesn't mean people sometimes don't pay their taxes, however, does it?"

"Well, no."

"So it is a law that people are supposed to pay taxes, but no one has to, if he or she is willing to run the risk of getting in trouble with the government."

"I'm not willing to run that risk." Alan chuckled.

"Me either," I said. "But let's move this now from a question of legality to a question of personal standards. When the United States went to war against Mexico, Henry David Thoreau was so against it, he refused to pay his taxes. He was supposed to pay his taxes, but he didn't have to. He chose, instead, to face the consequences. He was arrested and put into jail.

"Thoreau's friend, Ralph Waldo Emerson, was also very much against the war in Mexico, but because Emerson believed in the democratic government of the United States in which the rule of the majority is to be obeyed, he paid his taxes. He *didn't have to*, but he chose to.

"One day, Emerson went to visit Thoreau in jail. He looked through the bars and asked, 'Henry, good friend, what are you doing in there?' to which Thoreau immediately replied, 'A better question, Emerson, is what are *you* doing out *there!*' "

Alan nodded his head. "I see your point. Both men had a choice, but no matter which choice they made, it would bring consequences with it. Thoreau chose to disobey the government and he wound up in jail. Emerson obeyed the government, but at the expense of his personal beliefs about the war."

"Exactly! The issue is not that one man was right or wrong in what he did. That isn't our concern. The only thing we are concerned with here is that both men did have options. So if Thoreau were here today in my office telling me he had to go to jail, you and I would know that just wasn't true. He did not have to go to jail. He chose to accept that option."

"Just like I didn't have to marry Sandra," Alan said, seeing the personal connection. "I just chose that option because it fit who I am and what I want to stand for the best."

"That's right," I said. "It was your choice. And to be angry at Sandra about something you chose to do isn't really honest or fair, is it?"

He shook his head. "I guess I've been using her as a scapegoat. I just didn't want to take responsibility for the choice I made. I suddenly feel like a real coward. I've been hiding behind my wife, using her as a shield against being responsible. I can see that there are a lot of things I blame for how I feel, especially when it comes to my marriage."

"I know these new insights are painful for you, Alan, and that the changes you need to make seem a long way off. But you are already on your way and further along toward taking responsibility for your life than a lot of people get."

At this point in our work together, Alan has taken more responsibility for his decision than ever before, but he occasionally lapses into a "look what you made me do" assault on Sandra. Now, he sees his resentment toward Sandra as a struggle to see the truth more clearly. And struggle he does. As Munger so accurately put it, "All truth is an achievement." This was certainly true in Alan's case. Seeing that he didn't have to marry Sandra and that he was responsible for his choice to do so was probably the toughest achievement of his life.

I hope you will take the discussion in this chapter seriously. More than a few of us walk around with hundreds of "have to's" dominating our thoughts, and, much like Alan, feel pretty bitter toward people, and life in general, for what we feel they are making us do. We feel like victims, not victors. Alan had certainly built a huge case for what a helpless victim he was regarding his marriage, and he had a ton of bitterness and resentment to show for it.

The truth we all need to see is that we don't have to do anything. That is how free we are. Seeing this leads to more acceptance of personal responsibility for what we choose to do in life and, consequently, a lot less bitterness and resentment.

A quick final thought. If you want certain "outcomes" in your life, you can legitimately argue there are "have to's." If you want a healthy body, you have to exercise and diet. If you want a mature marriage, you have to spend time attending to it. If you want stable employment, you pretty much have to go to work consistently. But, remember, you don't have to want a healthy body, a mature marriage, or stable employment. The point here is that there are no real "have to's" until you choose to want some specific result or outcome in your life. Then, the "have to's" are real, but you are freely choosing them.

Try out the following statements and see how they sound:

"I choose to go to work."
"I choose to stay married."
"I choose to love my kids and raise them properly."
"I choose to lose weight."
"I choose to be unhappy (or happy) in my life."
"I choose to get angry at the guy who rides my bumper."
"I choose to let things from the past continue to hurt me."
"I choose to allow people to treat me the way that they do."
"I choose whether or not to have a satisfying life."

If these have the ring of truth to them, you are on your way to living a very healthy life. If they don't, you have a lot of work to do yet. Keep working, though, it will be worth it. It was for Alan.

DISCOVERING YOUR FREEDOM

I told you at the end of chapters 2 and 3 that I would show you additional ways to make use of your TRUTH journal. First, look back into previous journal entries and reexamine some of your trigger events. See if you told yourself you "had to" in the Unhealthy Response section of your entry. Look at how your feelings and actions were impacted by telling yourself this.

Now, for the next week, I want you to keep as accurate a record as you can of all the times you tell yourself you "have to" do something about some situation in your life. Write down these statements and then use your TRUTH system to decide if you have options (which, as we have discovered in this chapter, you almost always will have), how many options there are, and what the potential consequences of each option will be. Based on what your journal reveals about these "have to" situations, try to decide what is the best choice available to you and then implement it.

For example, let's say someone at work who you don't like that much asks you to meet for lunch on a regular basis. Using the TRUTH system to examine this, your entries might look something like this:

(T)rigger Event: A woman I don't like that much asked me to meet with her for lunch on a regular basis.

(R)eflection: I have to meet with her or it will hurt her feelings. I can't really say no, even though that is what I really want to say. Why do people do this to me?

(U)nhealthy Response: I felt trapped, angry, resentful that she asked.

(T)ruth: I don't have to say yes to her. Her feelings might be hurt, but that really isn't my responsibility. I can tell her the truth, which is that I already have lunch partners. I could thank her for asking me to join her—it is a compliment that she likes me enough to have asked. I could try to eat with her

now and then, like once a month, just to show some kindness and interest. Whatever I do, it is a choice. I really don't have to say yes just because I was asked. I'll be honest and tell her that meeting regularly won't work for me but that I will be glad to meet with her once a month.

(H)ealthy Response: I feel less trapped, somewhat anxious about telling her no, but better about handling it this way.

The thrust of this assignment is to fight your "have to" mind-set with the truth that you have options and the freedom to choose from among them and to help you accept responsibility for what you decide to do. I encourage you to prove this truth in your life as often as you can. In the process, you will see more clearly than ever before that you don't have to be a victim in life or put up with the emotions that go along with being a victim.

CHAPTER 6

■

You Are Going to Die

Pale death with impartial tread beats
at the poor man's cottage door and at
the palaces of kings.

—Horace

F ew truths have the potential to affect our lives as
strongly as the one that warns, "You *are* going to
die." Death waits around the corner for us all. As Dr.
Irvin Yalom expressed in his book *Existential Psychotherapy,* "The most obvious, the most easily apprehended ultimate concern is death. We exist now, but
one day shall cease to be. Death will come, and there
is no escape from it. It is a terrible truth, and we respond to it with mortal terror."[1]

Death may be "a terrible truth," but it is a truth that
can be used positively to prompt us to live life more
fully. I'm not going to use "positive thinking" on you
and try to make you view death as a categorically
great and wonderful thing. However, I do hope to
strongly impress upon you that seeing death accurately can significantly change your way of living.
And facing the truth about death can change you in
other ways too.

At the risk of stating the obvious, death is the ultimate limitation placed on life. Dr. Dennis E. Hensley explained succinctly in his book *How to Manage Your Time* how mankind has sought for centuries, in a variety of ways, to extend the time we have on earth; yet death always wins and in an amazingly predictable way:

> We are all destined for a guaranteed termination. No one has ever beaten the system. In fact, the Bible even tells us about how long we have before our termination: three score and ten (Psalm 90:10). It's interesting to note that even though that calculation was recorded three millennia ago, it hasn't changed. After thirty centuries of medical, educational, social and scientific advances, research conducted annually by insurance companies reveals that the average person lives to be from seventy to seventy-five years old (three score and ten). Every moment of life is valuable. Once time is gone, it's gone forever. You can't buy it back, borrow it back, bribe it back, or even pray it back. A wasted moment is irretrievable.[2]

The above quotation underscores the truth that you are going to die. It even helps us to know about when it may happen. The limitation death places on life makes our time here important. The fact that life comes in limited quantities can be used to motivate us to lead quality lives. Because of the reality of death, we are pushed to see life as something precious and, thus, to live accordingly.

Now, before you get too self-assured that you are already time-conscious and leading a quality-filled life, let me share some statistics with you. If you get eight hours of sleep a night, you will spend approximately 122 days a year sleeping. If you spend one hour each for breakfast, lunch, and dinner every day, you will spend 47 days a year in these activities alone. Sleeping and eating combined cost you half of each year you are alive. Add to that all the time spent in personal grooming, travel to and from work, bill paying, shopping and other life maintenance requirements, and you can see how much time "slips away" virtually undetected.

With what time we do have left for making life meaningful, we often find ourselves going through the motions and achieving very little of lasting value.

I once heard a story of a man who was driving by an apple orchard when he happened to see a farmer lifting his pigs, one at a time, up to the tree branches so that the pigs could eat the apples. The man stopped his car, got out, and approached the farmer. "Excuse me," he said, "but isn't that an awfully time-consuming practice?" The farmer looked at the man, shrugged his shoulders, and said, "So what? What's time to a pig?"

I sometimes wonder if a lot of people are just as blind as the farmer when it comes to recognizing areas in their lives where they are squandering time.

HAVING THE TIME OF YOUR LIFE

The fact that placing a limitation on something often makes it more valuable came through loud and clear to me during a recent vacation. My wife, Holly, and I took a trip to Jamaica prior to the birth of our third child. (It was one of those "we'd better go have some fun *now* while we still can" kind of vacations.) While there, I decided to ride a jet ski, which was something I had never done. The rate I had to pay the hotel concession was $30 per half hour of riding time. That struck me as being pretty expensive, but I paid it anyway.

With the time limitation of just thirty minutes hanging over me, I tried to get as much enjoyment out of that ride as I could. I rode at all different speeds, turned the sharpest corners I could turn, tried to cross as much of the ocean bay as possible, and even purposely fell off a few times just to increase the excitement.

All during the ride I constantly kept an eye on my watch, knowing that my time would be up relatively soon. I knew the rental guys would frantically start to wave me in as soon as the thirty minutes were over. This time constraint motivated me to try to squeeze all the enjoyment possible from that ride.

Now, suppose when I had registered at the hotel I had been told that I was the one millionth customer to have booked a reservation, and as a prize for this, I was going to be given unlimited time on a jet ski during all the days I was in Jamaica. Do you think I would have found it as intense and challenging and exciting to ride a jet ski under those circumstances? No, not hardly.

I'm convinced the same principle applies to life. Those who truly recognize and respect that life has a time limit will make an effort to get the best ride they can. They will experience life fully and will appreciate what is available to them.

If death can motivate us to maximize our time, it can be seen in a positive light. If there were no death and everyone just stayed on the planet forever, do you think people would have a sense of urgency about anything? Would the experience of life be as intense? Would we work as hard to enjoy it? For most of us, the answer would be "Probably not."

All right then, we will accept death as a prime motivator for life. But that raises a serious question: Why aren't people being motivated to have a fuller life if they know their days are numbered? More specifically, how can so many people mope along at a mediocre, unexciting pace or fill their lives with meaningless busy work when they know that their time is running out? Hey, let's face it: Life is not a dress rehearsal—this is the real thing. Lights, camera, action! You're *on*, friend! This is your life. You have the starring role. It's either an Oscar or obscurity. The choice is yours.

So why isn't everybody shooting for an Oscar? I think people are so terrified by the prospect of death, they will do anything to avoid facing dying. Like children who put their hands over their ears and say over and over, "I'm not listening, I'm not listening, I'm not listening," these adults say, "I'm not acknowledging the truth of death, I'm not acknowledging the truth of death." The more terrified people are of the concept of death, the more they will stay preoccupied with "things to do" rather than live with purpose and fullness.

WHEN DEATH HAPPENS

Woody Allen once remarked, "I'm not afraid of death. I just don't want to be there when it happens."

Too many of us feel that same way. But death awaits us all. As we've said, rather than face the reality of death, many of us numb ourselves to it in one way or another. Some of us try to ignore it through busyness, others try to laugh it away. Some try to postpone it, others try to outsmart it. Nothing works, however. Death always claims its final victory.

For a long time my own version of avoiding the reality of death (and trying to improve a shaky sense of self-esteem) was to be a workaholic. Like people we referred to earlier, I, too, thought that death wouldn't have a way to invade my consciousness if I just kept myself constantly busy. You may have done something similar, or you may have used some other way of running from this "terrible truth." I can tell you this, however: Your way of running is no more successful than mine was. Death still waits. Refusing to face it as something real often results in a less than fulfilled life.

The inevitability of death can motivate us to attempt to live a more minute-by-minute intensive existence. Knowing death is pending can actually challenge us to spend our days well. If we spend our lives well, death loses much of its sting. As Leonardo da Vinci put it, "As a well-spent day brings happy sleep, so life well used brings happy death."

Given that our time on earth is relatively short, how then shall we use it?

WHEN DEATH BECOMES REAL

How many times have you heard about a person who came close to death and used that experience as a springboard to a more meaningful and enjoyable life? A man might almost be killed in an airplane crash and, by facing death so squarely, come to appreciate and savor life more fully. A woman may be told she has a life-threatening cancer but, thanks to a successful operation, survives. Afterward, she quits her job as a sales clerk and becomes a teacher because she finds it more rewarding. A rebellious teenager may be involved in a near fatal car accident, yet walk away; afterward, he has a new sense of the value of life and he becomes more meaningfully involved in high-school activities and community service.

It could be that our unwillingness to accept death under normal circumstances is what makes near-death experiences so life changing. Nevertheless times of crisis enable people to see what life is really all about. American author Jack London traveled to the Yukon hoping to make a gold strike and come home a rich man. He staked one claim, but it held no gold. When winter came, London was unable to leave the Klondike because of the heavy snows. He spent four months in a cabin, often by himself, waiting for the spring thaw. He had a lot of time to reflect on his random style of living: He had been an oyster pirate in San Francisco, a seal hunter off the coasts of Japan and Russia, a factory worker, a hobo, a high-school drop-out. It began to bother him greatly that he had been busy, but he had done nothing significant with his life.

That spring Jack London left Canada, came home, finished his high-school work, spent a semester at the University of California, then turned all his energies toward becoming a writer. During the next 18 years, London wrote 190 short stories, 22 novels, 5 plays, 28 poems, and more than 200 newspaper articles. He became the first person in history to earn more than a million dollars strictly from writing.

When asked to summarize what motivated him to his huge success as a writer, Jack London said that when he was trapped in the Yukon he developed a credo which he swore would guide him for the rest of his life. His credo was as follows: "I would rather be a superb meteor, every atom of me in magnificent glow, than a sleepy and permanent planet. The proper function of man is to live, not just exist. I shall not waste my days in trying to prolong them. I shall use my time." Jack London knew the reality of death and so he used each day to its fullest.

Pretty amazing, isn't it? Jack London went from being a high-school drop-out with no money to becoming the most successful author the world had known to that time because he was forced to acknowledge that his days on earth were limited. And he did it all in just eighteen years. That's not a bad trade-off: four lonely months snowbound in a northern cabin in exchange for eighteen years of unbridled success.

What about you? Do you know what you specifically want out of life? Do you know why you are working as hard as you are? Do you know what you value most? Take a moment right now to fill out the checklist on page 73 called "Ranking Your Priorities." If, like Jack London, you had only eighteen more years to live, which items would you rate as "essential"?

RANK YOUR PRIORITIES

		Essential to have	Important to have after essentials	Expendable in a pinch	Totally frivolous
1.	Living in a nice apartment in a nice neighborhood				
2.	Owning a nice home in a nice neighborhood				
3.	Continuing the husband's education				
4.	Continuing the wife's education				
5.	Putting aside money for the children's educations				
6.	Buying a better car				
7.	Buying a second car				
8.	Owning a boat, motorcycle, camper or other RV				
9.	Buying new clothes each season				
10.	Buying household appliances and furnishings				
11.	Remodeling the home				
12.	Saving for retirement				
13.	Regular saving for any purpose				
14.	Eating out once a week				
15.	Entertaining at home on a regular basis				
16.	Going to movies, the theater and concerts regularly				

17. Travel				
18. Buying stocks or other investments				
19. Buying insurance				
20. Buying books and records regularly				
21. Subscribing to magazines and newspapers				
22. Owning a color television				
23. Owning an expensive stereo				
24. Owning an air conditioner				
25. Buying art and antiques				
26. Paying for a hobby				
27. Attending sporting events regularly				
28. Belonging to a country club or health club				
29. Contributing to charities, special causes or political campaigns				
30. Buying expensive Christmas, birthday and other gifts				

YOUR PERSONAL AWAKENING

In early 1991 a motion picture starring Robert De Niro and Robin Williams called *Awakenings* was released. It told the story of a physician who used a drug to bring people out of a physical disorder referred to as "sleeping sickness." De Niro played the part of a man who had gone into a coma-like sleep when he was in his twenties and was brought back to consciousness in his late forties. When De Niro fully realized what had happened to his life, he began frantically seeking to make up for lost time. He read books, went dancing, played sports, and even found himself a girlfriend. Moviegoers watching his antics experienced conflicting emotions: On the one hand they are delighted that this man is well again and so excited about life; on the other hand they are uneasy about the fact that his life is no further behind than theirs— *only they haven't been in a coma!*

I wonder sometimes if it would not be good for most of us to have a near-death or a Rip Van Winkle experience so that we could have a personal awakening. Consider this: Russel Noyes reported in *Psychiatry* magazine that after studying the lives of two hundred people who had undergone near-death experiences, 23 percent felt the ordeal had helped them discover more of what life was all about.[3] They said they learned that life was brief and precious and this realization gave greater zest to their lives. They also said they had heightened perceptions of their immediate surroundings and, hence, had greater emotional responsivity to all living things. They learned to live in the moment and to savor time. They developed an urge to enjoy as much as possible before it was too late.

These findings coincide with work psychiatrist Irvin Yalom did with terminally ill cancer patients. Yalom reported that once his patients accepted the fact that their lives were rapidly drawing to an end, significant changes in priorities and behavior became evident along the following lines:

- A rearrangement of life's priorities; a trivializing of the trivial.

- A sense of liberation; being able to choose not to do those things they did not wish to do.
- An enhanced sense of living in the immediate present, rather than postponing good times until after retirement or some other point in the future.
- A vivid appreciation of the elemental facts of life: the changing seasons, a fresh breeze, autumn leaves turning colors, and holiday joyousness.
- Deeper communication with loved ones.
- Fewer interpersonal fears, less concern about rejection, and greater willingness to take risks.[4]

It's sad to admit, isn't it, that most of us would have to go through a near-death experience before we could begin to appreciate life at its best? We really don't know what we've got until we almost lose it. Norman Cousins aptly stated, "Death is not the greatest loss in life. The greatest loss in life is what dies inside of us while we live."

Tolstoy's short story, "The Death of Ivan Ilyich," brings out a point about the difference between "going through" life and actually living life to the fullest. Ivan Ilyich is a sour and evil fellow. He develops cancer and begins to suffer greatly. As he endures his agony, he comes to a life-changing realization: *He is dying badly because he has lived badly.* The recognition of this truth alters Ivan Ilyich's whole perspective on life, and he makes radical changes in his personality and his way of living. He starts to see life as valuable and he attempts to make the maximum use of whatever time he has left.

THE SCROOGE SYNDROME

As we draw this chapter to an end, I'm going to walk you through an activity that can help motivate you to make the most of the time you have left to live. Let me preface the explanation by reminding you of Charles Dickens's classic story *A Christmas Carol*. You will recall that Ebenezer Scrooge spent his life in a miserly, selfish, lonely existence. All he cared about was accumulating and hoarding money.

Then one Christmas Eve a supernatural thing occurred: Scrooge was visited by three ghosts. One ghost made him recall his past and forced him to confront the fact that he had once had good friends and the love of a beautiful young lady, but his greed had driven them all away.

The second ghost made Scrooge take a revealing look at the present. He saw starving children, overworked laborers, and destitute beggars whom he passed without seeing every day on his way to work. He saw the family of his employee Bob Cratchit. Bob's youngest son, Tiny Tim, was dying because the family lacked money for proper medical care for the boy. If Scrooge had ever had an ounce of concern, he would have known of the situation; but he was always too occupied counting his gold and reviewing the ledgers.

The third ghost showed Scrooge the immediate future. Not only was Tiny Tim going to die, but so, too, was Scrooge. After his death, people were going to ransack his house and mock his memory. Everyone would rejoice over his death. No one would put flowers on his grave.

Naturally, all this terrified old Ebenezer. He recognized that he had wasted his life in petty, lonely, small-minded activities.

As you know, the story has a happy ending. Scrooge was given a second chance. Instead of dying, he was allowed to go on living for several more years. Scrooge set to work immediately to make up for lost time. He bought food for the poor; he donated money to the needy; he paid a visit to his nephew's home; and he gave Bob Cratchit a raise that doubled his salary. All this change in his character made him "as giddy as a school boy." We are left with the feeling that Scrooge probably did more *living* during the last years of his life than he did in all the previous sixty years.

Now, I want you to have the same experience. Look at the "Life Map" found in this chapter. I want you to fill it out.

In the box at the bottom of the page, you need to write in today's date. Then jot down some of the accomplishments of your life, such as "high-school graduate," "two years in U.S. army," "married eleven years," "two terrific children," "elected church deacon," "four bowling trophies," "completely rebuilt a 1965 Mustang," "became store assistant manager in 1992." Make a note of whatever you are proud of having achieved in life thus far.

Then, go up to the next box and write in what the date will be exactly one year from today. In that box, write down three or four things that would greatly enrich your life if you were to accomplish them between today and one year from today. You might jot down "read a dozen classic works of literature" or "attend a seminar on money management" or "start a sideline business in antique jewelry" or "take a class

LIFE MAP

X RETIREMENT

(Write a Who's Who entry about your life and accomplishments.)

Date:
My Goal:

Thirty Years
From Now

Date:
My Goal:

Fifteen Years
From Now

Date:
My Goal:

Five Years
From Now

Date:
My Goal:

Three Years
From Now

Date:
My Goal:

One Year
From Now

(Write a summary of your
accomplishments to date.)

X STARTING
   POINT

Date:

in real estate" or "learn to read music and play the piano." Consider these to be your goals for the coming year.

Continue to move up the boxes, filling in the dates three, five, fifteen, and thirty years from today. Stretch your imagination. What would you like to do, like to be, like to experience, like to learn, like to share, like to see, and like to try during those years?

Finally, like Scrooge, try to leap (via your imagination) to the end of your life. Once you are dead, what will people remember about you? What will your obituary say? What would a *Who's Who* entry about you read like at the end of your life? Put these dreams and goals of yours into a short list in the top box. You might say, "became a millionaire" or "won a seat in congress" or "wrote a best-selling novel" or "discovered a cure for AIDS" or "was named Teacher of the Year" or "visited 65 different countries" or "discovered a rare archeological dig." Put down on paper your greatest ambitions.

Now, here is a gift more valuable than you may have ever stopped to appreciate: You get to go on living. You have something worth more than anything imaginable—life! You have time—time to reach your goals and to fulfill your dreams. Yes, one day you are going to die. That painful truth can't be escaped by any of us. But, today, it really is lights, camera, action! You are being asked to step out on stage and give your best effort. You have the gift of life to use as meaningfully and abundantly as possible. With all that you have in you try to give life your best shot. Remember, pale death beats at your death.

CHAPTER 7

■

The Virtue Lies in the Struggle, Not the Prize[1]

When the one Great Scorer comes to write against your name, he marks not that you won or lost, but how you played the game.

—Grantland Rice

One day two ladies met on the street.

"Lucy, I haven't seen you in ages," said the first lady. "Your new pet store must really be keeping you busy."

"All the animals got sick from bad water," said Lucy. "They died and I lost the business."

"My word! How tragic. You and Ralph must be heartbroken."

"Ralph is dead. One of the dogs bit him and he contracted rabies. Didn't last a month."

"Incredible," said the first woman. "Your son must miss him terribly."

"The shock was too much for him. He died of a heart attack."

"Your son too? This is just too much to believe. How dreadful!"

"Oh, but wait," said Lucy, starting to smile, "you haven't heard the good news yet . . . ."

And just then a bolt of lightning struck her and she fell dead on the sidewalk.

We all might laugh at this story, not because we enjoy sick humor but because we all can identify so strongly with the poor lady's problems. As you face each day, it can seem as though life is one problem after another. On Monday your electric bill arrives and it's three times as much as you have left in your bank account. On Tuesday your child comes down with strep throat. On Wednesday your car dies so you have to start bumming a ride until it's fixed. On Thursday your spouse tells you he or she is sick and tired of being married. On Friday you discover you have lost thousands of dollars in a poor stock investment.

And so it goes, never ending.

Maybe that's why we laugh so hard when we watch Wile E. Coyote in his continuous efforts to catch the Road Runner. It's like watching ourselves. When something goes wrong for the coyote, it usually leads to a chain reaction of catastrophes. The boulder he rolls down the hill at the Road Runner circles up the opposite wall and comes back down and smashes poor Wile E. . . . and then the cliff ledge he is on gives way and he drops down the canyon and smashes into the ground . . . after which, the same boulder falls on him again. Finally, he squeezes from under the boulder, staggers to his feet, only to be run over by a passing truck.

It's so stupid, yet for thirty-plus years I've watched those cartoons and laughed my sides out. It's fun. It's fun because even though we see the coyote squashed into an accordion, we know that ten seconds later he will be up and ready to try something new.

There's a message in that. When we're laughing at that ridiculous coyote, we're laughing at ourselves, at the way we are, at the way life is. Pursuing the Road Runner is what gives meaning to Wile E. Coyote's life. Catching and eating the scrawny little bird would almost seem anticlimactic after all those years of scheming and plotting for his capture. After the conquest, what next? It's the struggle that brings out the persistence and drive and ingenuity of the coyote. That's what makes us laugh—he's always getting smarter because he just doesn't know when to quit.

And neither do we, I hope.

There's a lot of human nature in Wile E. Coyote. We often love a struggle even more than the prize it offers us. It has always been that way. When Alexander the Great conquered the entire known world in 323 B.C., he sat down and wept. There were no more battles to be won. Nearly three thousand years later, just months after the July 20, 1969, date when Edwin "Buzz" Aldrin, Jr., became one of the first two men to walk on the moon, Aldrin realized that, as a pilot, there were no greater achievements he could strive for in his lifetime, and he had a nervous breakdown.

One of the great ironies of life is that people complain constantly about how hard it is to "get ahead"; yet when they no longer have to struggle, they seem either to go "stir crazy" and *make* work for themselves or they lose their inner sense of purpose in life and develop emotional problems. Few people seem able to "stand success" and enjoy the "prize" once they have it. The inability to enjoy the struggle along the way makes enjoying the prize difficult, if not impossible, for many of us.

This has been one of the recurrent themes of great

literature throughout the ages. Throughout the novel *Les Misérables*, by Victor Hugo, a police inspector named Javert hunts the elusive criminal Jean Valjean. In the end, when Javert finally has a chance to capture and arrest Valjean after many years of pursuit, he cannot bring himself to do it. Instead, he hurls himself into the Seine River, committing suicide. The chase had given him a reason for living. For it to end was for life to end.

Consider the real-life parallels to that. Have you ever heard parents say that they can't wait to get their kids raised and out of the house so that they can have some time to themselves . . . yet once the kids are gone these same parents nearly go crazy with all the time they have on their hands?

Have you ever heard a man say he couldn't wait until retirement so that he wouldn't have to work any longer, yet once retirement came he became depressed, maybe even suicidal, because he lost his work-related identity? This was one of the themes in Joseph Waumbaugh's novel *The New Centurions*, which relates the story of a police officer who killed himself after he was retired from the force because he no longer felt he had a reason to exist.

I have had my own struggles with the virtue lies in the struggle not the prize truth. My own tendency is to be so "prize-minded" that my efforts along the way get little or no credit. Graduate school felt like that. I felt as if contentment and "victory" were only to be obtained when I got my doctorate, not in my efforts to get it. Five years of graduate school was a long time to postpone victory. Writing my first book, *The Lies We Believe*, was the same way. I worked hard for over a year to write it, but I didn't allow myself many feelings of accomplishment until it was done. The effort to write it seemed to have no virtue to it, whereas the actual "prize" of finishing the book is where I put so much of my sense of victory.

In each case, I cost myself a great deal. In retrospect, I can see that the virtue was in the effort to finish a doctorate, not getting one. I can also see that the virtue was in the effort to write a book, not in its finally coming out. This "scoreboard" mentality, where the effort on the field is considered less important than the final score, crushes a lot of us.

Although we spend our whole lives denying it by focusing on the prize, the truth is that the virtue lies in the struggle of trying to achieve something, not in finally earning the reward dangled before us for so long.

ACCEPTING THE STRUGGLE

There is another "spin" on this issue of pursuing a dream we have to grapple with: not achieving it. How many times have you felt like a loser because something you were earnestly trying to accomplish didn't come through? So many times in life, our efforts don't result in what we hoped they would. The salesperson invests tremendous amounts of time in making an important sale to somebody and it doesn't come through. The athlete trains diligently for a major competition yet doesn't place in the top three. Parents put their "all" into raising respectable children, yet one of them goes out and makes numerous unwise decisions that go in the face of how he or she was raised. Life is full of these kinds of situations where our efforts aren't rewarded with a successful outcome, or at least aren't as successful as we had hoped.

In situations like these, most of us would feel as though we had failed and that there was no value in our efforts. Our struggle would not feel worthwhile to us unless it was rewarded with the prize we were after. As before, let me suggest that the truth we need to face is that the virtue is always in our efforts, not in what they yield.

Yes, I know this sounds trite, but if understood on a deeper level, this truth becomes very important. It creates more willingness to try and less resentment and bitterness if your efforts do not turn out so well. Let me take you into the counseling office again to show you just how important this truth is.

Hal was a full-blown perfectionist, which caused chronic feelings of depression and low self-esteem for him. Throughout his life, he struggled with a feeling that his performance was never good enough. In college he made grades that most of us would rejoice over, but to him they were mediocre because he didn't make all A's all the time.

He felt the same way about his performance in sports. He was an avid golfer, but he was chronically upset about his golf game because it was never "good enough." He might shoot the best round of his life yet walk away upset because of the one or two holes he played imperfectly.

In our sessions together, Hal started to accept the to err is human truth discussed earlier in this book, and his depression and self-hatred began to lessen. However, in spite of this progress, Hal started to feel that his improvement should be coming faster. He wasn't going to be satisfied until he had his perfectionism cured. So we discussed this.

"Dr. Thurman, I'm getting very impatient with therapy. Things aren't going fast enough to suit me. I'm not getting better quickly enough!"

"You feel you should be changing faster?" I asked.

"Yes. I feel like I should be over this problem by now," he answered, as if not wanting to be challenged on it.

"Hal, it sounds to me like you're being perfectionistic about your perfectionism," I said.

"What! What do you mean by that?"

"Well, you have been perfectionistic since the time you were a very young boy, practicing it day by day for more than forty years, and after twelve sessions of therapy you feel as though you should be cured. How realistic is that?"

"Not very, I guess," Hal admitted. "But I can't really feel good about things until I whip this thing."

I shook my head slowly. "No virtue in the effort, just the prize," I mumbled, more to myself than to Hal.

"What's that?" Hal asked. "I'm not sure what you mean by that."

"You seem to take no satisfaction from the fact that you are trying to fight your perfectionism. Instead, you've decided to believe that you can't claim victory until you completely defeat your problem."

"Well, that's true, isn't it? Until I defeat my perfectionism, there is no victory."

"I don't agree with you," I said bluntly. "The fact that you came here for help and are trying to be less perfectionistic is your real victory, your 'virtue,' if you will. It's not a matter of whether or not you've beaten it yet."

"That sounds nice in theory," he shot back, "but while I'm still struggling with perfectionism, I'm continuing to be depressed, angry, and unhappy. That isn't much of a reward for all this work I've been doing."

"But you're doing all that you can. Can't that be enough?" I asked, knowing full well that Hal wouldn't see it that way.

"No, it isn't enough. I'm not going to be content until I see some results for my efforts. That's just the way I am about things."

"But I thought 'the way you are about things' was why you'd been so unhappy and why you came in for help," I countered. "You sound like you're making a case for staying the way you are."

"No, I'm just saying that it's hard for me to accept mere 'effort' as the *victory*. What I want is the end result—that's the victory I'm after."

"I understand that, Hal, but I think this attitude is what often gets you into emotional trouble. So many times the reward for our efforts is way down the road, if available at all. In light of that, it seems to me that our effort to try to accomplish something worthwhile has to be the victory."

"Maybe, but what you want me to accept is pretty foreign to my whole way of thinking," said Hal. "I'm not sure I can buy into it."

"Believe me, I know what you are talking about. The idea that the effort is the key thing didn't always fit into my way of thinking either. But I believe it to be one of the critical truths we need to live by while we struggle to be emotionally healthy. Given that you play golf, let me put it this way. The virtue is not actually in breaking par but in making an effort to play your best. As simple as that sounds, it is the truth."

"So you are telling me to fight my perfectionism by letting my efforts to change be enough—at least for now—and to quit focusing so much on whether or not I make a total change. That, I guess, will come by making the effort, right? Sort of like playing golf: Just work on keeping your head down and left arm straight and the ball almost *has* to fly in the direction you want it to."

"Yes, that's right," I agreed. "All we can do is make the effort. That is your victory, your virtue. Then the ball goes where it goes."

BEATING THE PERFECTION SYNDROME

Hal is doing much better as of this writing, but it has taken him a long time to find out why he felt the need to be perfect. Part of it was a carryover from his childhood.

When Hal was a youngster, his father used to take him out for a hamburger and a malt whenever he would hit a home run or play well during a game. However, on nights when Hal played poorly, his father drove him straight home. From this, Hal surmised that he was not accepted and of no value to his father unless he played "great." Hal's whole life might have been different if his father had said things like, "I'm sorry you struck out, son, but I'm proud of you anyway because you did your best. Let's go grab a burger and then get home in time to play a little catch before it gets dark."

As a youngster, Hal needed his parents' help to understand that to err is human and to see that his parents had *unconditional* love for him. He needed to know he was loved whether he played well or poorly, won or lost. Since he was not given an understanding of either of these points, he fell victim to the Vince Lombardi mania that says, "Winning isn't everything, it's the *only* thing." What rubbish.

Here's a better perspective for you to have on winning and losing. Teddy Roosevelt was shorter than most men. He had poor eyesight. As a child, he was often quite sick. He was married in 1880 to Alice Hathaway Lee, who died just four years later. He ran for mayor of New York City and lost. He ran for president in 1912 and lost. He organized an expedition in 1919 to explore the remote jungles of South America but died of a blood clot before getting very far into the jungle.

At a quick glance, it would seem that Teddy Roosevelt had a terrible life. But Roosevelt lived daily by the concept that the virtue lies in the struggle, not the prize. Here is how he expressed it:

> The credit belongs to the man who is actually in the arena; whose face is marred by dust and sweat; who strives valiantly; who errs and may fail again and again, because there is no effort without error or shortcoming; but who does actually strive to do the deeds, who knows the great enthusiasm, the great devotion.[2]

Did this attitude help Roosevelt through those terrible phases of his life? You be the judge. Here is a brief summary of his life's accomplishments: commissioner of the New York City Police; assistant secretary of the

U. S. Navy; colonel in the Rough Riders; governor of New York; vice president of the United States in 1900; at age forty-two, the youngest man ever to serve as president of the United States (1901–1909); author of two thousand published articles, essays, and books; father of six children in two marriages; winner of the Nobel Peace Prize in 1906.

Teddy Roosevelt was a "winner" every day of his life—whether he won an election or lost it, whether he made progress on a task or suffered a setback—because Roosevelt's personal definition of a "winner" was someone who made an effort. Making the effort and being "on the field" was what counted, not if you finished win, place or show.

WHEN LOSING IS WINNING

Champions in sports, business, politics, industry, and the arts know this truth: If you do your best at something, you end up the winner even if the scoreboard says you've lost.

I realize that sounds contradictory, but stay with me a moment and I'll show you how it works.

During the 1980 Olympics, an American athlete named Eric Heiden took all five gold medals for men's speed skating. In the first four events Heiden set new Olympic speed records: 38.03 seconds for the 500-meter race; 1 minute 15.18 seconds for the 1000-meter; 1 minute 55.44 seconds in the 1500-meter; and 7 minutes 2.29 seconds in the 5000-meter.

In the final event, the 10,000-meter race, Heiden not only broke the Olympic record, he also set a new all-time world speed record of 14 minutes 28.13 seconds.

As amazing as these victories were, they came as no

surprise to those who had followed Eric Heiden through the years. Heiden had been winning every time he competed in an amateur race. He was recognized as the greatest men's speed skater who had ever lived. Sports writers knew it; coaches knew it; even Heiden's competitors knew it. The plain and simple fact was, no one could equal Eric Heiden when it came to speed skating.

Now, you may think that such knowledge would demoralize and deflate people who had to compete against Heiden. After all, what was the point of entering a race when you knew in advance you had no chance whatsoever of equaling the champion? Depressing, right?

Just the opposite proved true. When Heiden won the 500-meter race, silver medal, second place honors went to Evgeni Kulikov of the USSR, *who turned in his personal fastest time ever* for the 500-meter race. When Heiden won the 1000-meter race, the runner-up was Gaetan Boucher of Canada, *who clocked his personal fastest time ever* in the 1000-meter.

And so it continued in every race. The silver and bronze medalists who lost to Heiden actually achieved greater personal speeds than ever before, simply because they were doing their best to be the equal of Eric Heiden. This phenomenon became known as the "Heiden Effect," which now is defined as achieving new personal victories by striving to equal a competitor one knows he can never be equal to or surpass.

Would you call Evgeni Kulikov and Gaetan Boucher a couple of losers just because they finished second to Eric Heiden? Not me. My feeling is that any person who exceeds all of his or her personal best levels of performance is a *winner*, no matter what the scoreboard says. That is the way I am trying to bring up my three children. If they make a solid effort, they'll be winners in my opinion. And unlike Hal's father, I plan to let my children *know* that their dad thinks they are winners—unconditionally!

The virtue lies in the struggle, not the prize. Memorize that truth. Meditate on it. Keep it available for those times you are working diligently on something and the reward is nowhere in sight. When you are fighting a weight problem and not making much progress, remind yourself the effort to lose weight is your victory. When you are fighting being in financial debt, remind yourself that the effort to pay off your bills is your virtue. If your marriage is faltering and all your efforts to make it better seem to be failing, remind yourself that your struggle to make the marriage better is your victory. I hope "I tried" can become a satisfying statement for you. More often than not, it will result in "I accomplished," which is the prize most of us want.

A NEW WAY OF THINKING

This seventh chapter, as with the chapters preceding it, has challenged you to alter your traditional way of thinking about certain ideas, relationships, and concepts you've heard or experienced all your life. As a closing exercise, I'd like you to get a pencil and paper and write down lists of the advantages and disadvantages of thinking the "old" way versus thinking these "new" ways.

What are the advantages or disadvantages of thinking, "To err is stupid and inexcusable" as compared to thinking, "To err is human"? What difference does it make in your life to think, "Things should be different from how they are" versus thinking, "What should have happened did"? What are the pros and cons of thinking, "The virtue is in the struggle, not the prize"?

Let the results of your lists tell you which beliefs to keep and which to throw away and replace with something better.

CHAPTER 8

■

You Are Not Entitled

This is the true joy in life, the being used for a purpose recognized by yourself as a mighty one; the being thoroughly worn out before you are thrown on the scrap heap; the being a force of nature instead of a feverish, selfish little clod of ailments and grievances complaining that the world will not devote itself to making you happy.

—George Bernard Shaw

One of the most difficult attitude problems any counselor faces is that of "entitlement." Entitlement is an attitude of, "I'm owed." It is apparent in beliefs such as these:

"I'm a college graduate, so I deserve a high paying job."

"I've been good to my friends, so they owe me their loyalty."

"I am a senior citizen, so I deserve younger people's respect."

"We weren't put on this earth to suffer, so life owes me a break."

"I took care of my kids when they were young, so I am entitled to some special care from them when I grow old."

Our culture loves to foster these notions in us. During the 1970s McDonald's restaurants built an entire ad campaign around the slogan, "You *deserve* a break today." In the 1980s another ad campaign said, *"Pamper* yourself with Calgon." In the 1990s it was "You *owe* it to yourself to buy a Mercedes Benz." Society continues to bombard us with the message that we are such fantastic people, we are entitled to an equally fantastic way of living.

To some degree, we all have entitlement feelings. We carry around a sense of being owed for something we have done or for some wonderful trait we have. When we feel entitled we focus on what we are owed, not what we might need to give to others. It is a "one-way street" mind-set. When these feelings are strong and people don't meet our expectations, we often find ourselves bitter, resentful, and angry. Relationships can be (and often are) destroyed by feelings of entitlement.

Such was the case of Stan and Julie, a couple who came to see me because their marriage was in deep trouble. They had been married for just a year and were already contemplating a divorce. They both were extremely angry and bitter toward each other and felt that the other person was to blame for how bad their marriage had turned out. As I explored their feelings with them, I began to see just how strongly both of them felt entitled to certain things from the marriage.

"Julie never listens to what I have to say," Stan complained. "She wants to be heard, but she never wants to listen."

"That's not true," Julie replied defensively. "I'm more than happy to listen. It's Stan who's never willing to listen to what I have to say."

"Why *should* I listen to you?" snapped Stan. "All you ever do is attack me for not meeting your needs . . . as if anyone could! You take and take and take, but you never want to give back."

"Boy, this is the pot calling the kettle black. All you ever do is think about what you want and how you are going to get it," Julie fired back.

I lifted my hands.

"Time out for just a second. Both of you sound pretty angry at each other. You both seem to feel that something isn't being offered that you deserve."

"Well, I know I don't get what I deserve from Julie," Stan acknowledged. "I work hard all day, take care of the upkeep on both of our cars, mow the lawn, pay the bills . . . I do everything and she's not grateful."

"He's far worse," Julie countered. "I work all day, too, but I still do the washing and ironing and most of the cooking. But does he show any gratitude? Never!"

They glared at each other, unblinking.

"I think I see one of the main problems in your marriage," I said, as referee. "Both of you seem to have a pretty strong case of it."

"What are you talking about?" Julie asked.

"Well, it seems to me that both of you feel entitled to love and consideration from each other," I explained. "Both of you seem to believe that the other person is indebted to you for what you do. You *expect* special treatment as appropriate payment. Indirectly, you both are saying to each other, 'Because I did this for you, you must do that for me.'"

"So? What's wrong with that?" Stan asked, exasperated. "The whole world is based on 'I do this for you and you do that for me.' Give and take. You scratch my back and I'll scratch yours. Why shouldn't marriage be the same way?"

"Stan, a tit-for-tat approach to marriage doesn't work," I answered. "Feelings of 'I deserve' or 'I'm owed' only foster rebellion in one another."

"Dr. Thurman, I'm not sure what you mean. Are you saying that I don't deserve to be listened to if I listen to Julie?" Stan responded in his typical defensive manner.

"Yes, Stan, I am. If you listen to Julie, that does not entitle you to be listened to by her. It isn't your birthright to get something back just because you give something in your marriage."

"Then why would anybody in his right mind want to give anything in marriage?" Stan demanded to know.

"For love," I stated flatly. "And because it's the right thing to do."

"What!" Stan said, nearly gasping. "You're joking, right?"

"No joke," I assured him. "I'm suggesting you need to do things like listen to each other, help each other, and work for each other with no strings attached because it is the mature and healthy thing to do. Look what happens when the two of you don't: You rebel toward one another.

"I think it is human nature to rebel when we feel that people feel entitled to our doing things for them. We don't appreciate the lack of respect that conveys. You rebel toward one another to show that you don't have to do what the other expects. The response is childish, but it's typical.

"You both throw your personal versions of a temper tantrum, and everyone loses. Demand or feel entitled to 'something for something' from each other and you will continue to see the relationship suffer. The only relationships that really work are those where both partners do what is loving and right whether they get anything back or not."

"What if the other person doesn't do the same thing?" Stan kept pressing. "Wouldn't the marriage get out of balance fast?"

"Yes, it could, but would that be any worse than the situation you're already in? Most marriages based on *non*entitlement don't get out of balance. When both people are doing what needs to be done without feeling entitled to payback, the marriage usually stays on pretty solid ground. Taking a nonentitlement stance with each other usually fosters emotional health, cooperation, and mutual respect. Marriages based on 'something for something' (entitlement) are doomed from the start. They never work!" I stated adamantly, knowing how cut and dried it sounded.

"So you're saying that a lot of our marital problems come from feeling that we are owed each other's attention, love, help, and so on," Julie summarized. "You're saying our marriage is troubled because we feel entitled to things from each other when we really aren't. And because we approach each other that way, we end up rebelling toward one another."

"I'm saying that is one of the more critical elements in why your marriage has been so troubled, yes," I replied.

FACING THE FACTS

This was the first time Stan and Julie had been asked to look at the issue of entitlement in their marriage. It was a new concept for them and one that was hard to see at first. They continued in their old patterns of "I did this for you, so you should do this for me" for a while, but small changes did occur as time went on. They eventually came to see the truth that they were not entitled to each other's love, respect, loyalty, and help just because it was "payback" time. This truth helped them appreciate what the other person did in the marriage and they started to sense that their marriage could be saved and enriched. They rebelled less toward each other. Entitlement attitudes came close to destroying their marriage; nonentitlement attitudes helped to heal it.

How much entitlement do you walk around with in your life? I can see a fair amount of it in mine. I feel those "I deserve" feelings more often than I want to admit. Even in small things, I can see the problem. When I hold the door open for someone, I feel he or she owes me a "thank you" and I get disappointed, even upset, when I don't get one. In my marriage, I sometimes catch myself thinking, "Holly owes me this because I have done that for her."

Even with my kids, I run into it. If I go to a lot of trouble to make a day special for them, I can sometimes find myself thinking, "Okay, you kids owe me some good behavior, as well as your lifelong appreciation for what a neat dad I am." (Unfortunately, they are thinking, "We are so doggone cute, it must be a real privilege for dad to get to spend a day with such adorable kids as us. We are responsible for most of the old boy's joy in life. He really owes us a lot.")

It's human nature to feel entitled. This isn't pleasant for me to admit. But unless we do admit to having these feelings, we stay in denial about them and they continue to destroy us.

The painful truth is that we are not entitled to anything on this planet. We are not entitled to "life, liberty, and the pursuit of happiness," despite what the authors of the Declaration of Independence had to say. Nothing is our birthright!

Now, the good news. While we are owed nothing, it is perfectly fine to pursue what we want (within reason and emotional health). For example, we aren't owed our spouse's or parents' love, but it is fine to want it. We aren't owed a high paying job because we may have a diploma or a special talent, but it is okay to want a high paying job and to try to find one. We aren't owed a thank you for anything we do, but it is okay to want one and hope to get one.

Entitlement is a self-serving, one-way street attitude that creates bitterness and resentment in the people who feel entitled and in the people around them who don't like being treated that way. Before you move on to the next chapter, take a minute to examine your own entitlement assumptions. Have you fallen into this way of thinking? Toward whom or what do you harbor feelings of entitlement? How has it affected you emotionally? How has it affected your relationships?

Are you willing to try to let go of entitlement attitudes and feelings wherever they may be directed? My hope is that this chapter has helped you recognize your need for change in this area and that you will decide to change.

GAUGING YOUR ENTITLEMENT EXPECTATIONS

I have devised an "Entitlement Quiz" for you to take. For each of the fifteen statements, mark a number from one to seven which gauges your personal feeling about the statement (*one* being the most disagreement and *seven* being the most agreement).

ENTITLEMENT QUIZ

Please answer the questions below using the following scale:

1	2	3	4	5	6	7
Strongly Disagree			Neutral			Strongly Agree

Do not spend too much time on any one item. Also please respond in terms of how you really feel as opposed to how you think you should feel. Try to avoid using the neutral response if possible.

_____ 1. I deserve respect from others.

_____ 2. I demand good service in a restaurant.

_____ 3. My closest friends owe me loyalty.

_____ 4. I expect fairness from others.

_____ 5. I'm owed a good paying job for my abilities.

_____ 6. People should treat me the way I treat them.

_____ 7. When I do something nice for someone, I find that I secretly expect them to do something nice for me.

_____ 8. I deserve a "thank you" when I hold a door open for someone or let someone ahead of me in traffic.

_____ 9. People should listen to what I have to say.

_____ 10. I often feel "owed" for things I have done.

_____ 11. Other people have told me I expect too much.

_____ 12. All in all, I deserve a good life.

_____ 13. I am entitled to "life, liberty, and the pursuit of happiness."

_____ 14. I find myself getting angry inside when others don't do things for me they said they would do.

_____ 15. My children owe me cooperation and obedience for all the sacrifices I have made for them.

Add all of the numbers of your fifteen responses; then divide that total by fifteen. The number you are left with will show you on the scale how convinced you are that you are "entitled" to certain things.

If you score from one to four, you really are <u>not</u> <u>expecting much from other people</u> in the way of gratitude, approval, and response. As such, you probably won't be disappointed in life when such responses aren't forthcoming. If you score from five to seven, you are probably a person who is carrying a lot of internal anger over the fact that not enough people give you what you feel entitled to. If that is the case, you need to readjust your expectations the way Stan and Julie did. You need to remind yourself that you are "owed" nothing for all you do and that <u>people</u> <u>have the perfect freedom to fly in the face of what you</u> <u>want</u>. You need to remember that the challenge is to do things for people because it's healthy or mature or "right", not because you can earn "green stamps" that you can cash in whenever you want.

Painful as it is, *you are not entitled.* Don't let that truth get too far away from you in life.

CHAPTER 9

■

There Is No Gain Without Pain

> One cannot get through life without
> pain. What we can do is choose how
> to use the pain life presents to us.
> —Bernie Siegel

I magine what your reaction might be if you saw a feature story in your hometown newspaper tomorrow morning that read as follows:

New Psychosurgery Technique Developed! Personal Maturity Now Possible Without Any Effort

Unbelievable Press International (UPI)—Doctors at Happy Days Hospital in Nirvana, New York, have developed a new method of surgery that can create mental health and maturity for people in a matter of hours. The technique involves going in the patient's brain with a laser scalpel and removing all of the patient's faulty beliefs, expectations, and attitudes. The patients who have had the procedure have reported a total absence of depression, worry, anger, and guilt after awakening from the surgery. They have also reported feeling a strong acceptance of themselves and of others for the first time in their lives. Dr. I. M.

Deluded is the surgeon who developed the psychosurgery technique. He hails his discovery as, "What everyone has been looking for all along—all the benefits of mental health without any hard work!" Dr. Deluded has reported receiving thousands of calls from all over the world from people asking about the availability of the new surgery. He stated that within ten years it would be possible for the whole world to have undergone the technique and a new level of world peace and understanding to emerge.

That sounds pretty attractive, doesn't it? Just about everybody on the planet would love to undergo surgery by someone else that would free them from all of their distorted thinking and the emotional misery created by it (except for those of us in the mental health profession who would be put out of work). There's only one problem: There's no such thing as psychosurgery or anything else that can help you grow and mature without your putting forth some effort—often, painful effort.

The desire for effortless, pain-free methods of personal growth and improvement goes back in time a long way. One of the earliest treatments of mental disorders we know of was a practice in the Stone Age called trephening. Trephening involved using crude stone instruments to chip away an area of the skull of a mentally disturbed person. This opening presumably allowed the evil spirit that was causing the emotional problem to escape. Some primitive people actually appear to have survived the surgery and lived for many years afterward. While the approach was certainly not painless, it still fits into the category of something being done to people to change them for the better, as opposed to people doing something themselves to become better.

The early belief that mental illness was the result of possession by evil spirits also gave rise to exorcism as a mental health technique. Exorcisms varied considerably, but most involved prayer, noise making, and the use of concoctions that tasted horrible. Extreme cases involved making the body of the possessed person such an unpleasant place, the evil spirit would leave voluntarily.

Another technique used to treat mental disorders with external actions rather than internal treatments was the "circulating swing." This approach, used in the early 19th century, involved strapping a patient in a chair that could be spun around. The technique was believed to help bring the mentally disturbed person back to sound reasoning. Ahhh . . . if it were only that easy.

In our current age many still continue to search for methods of achieving emotional health that are easy and painless. Psychoactive medication is sometimes viewed that way. I have had more than a few patients come in just to have some pills prescribed to make their depression or anxiety go away, not really to work on the underlying issues causing these problems. When I informed them that I was a psychologist, not a psychiatrist who can prescribe medication, some quit coming back. They were convinced that a pill could make them whole. So they went off looking for the professional who would prescribe medication for their ills.

Please don't hear what I am saying as a blanket criticism of the use of medication in helping troubled people. Psychoactive medication has played an extremely important role in the fight against mental illness and will continue to. It's just that too many people seem to think that a pill (or something like it) can circumvent the painful, laborious work required in becoming mentally healthy people. This fantasy can be hard to kill.

NO QUICK-FIX SOLUTIONS

Dan, a patient of mine, was someone who truly wished for a quick-fix solution to all his emotional problems. He came to see me because of employment difficulties and the depression he felt about them. His marriage was also in bad shape, and his wife was very close to walking out on him.

For most of his life, Dan had been dodging his problems, hoping they would just go away. But now, in later years, the results of this dodging were beginning to catch up with him in some undeniable ways. One session we had began like this:

"Have a seat, Dan. What would you like to talk about today?"

Dan shrugged his shoulders.

"Oh, I don't know," he responded, as if he didn't care.

"Why don't you start with what seems to be bothering you most," I suggested.

"Well, I suppose I just still feel kind of depressed about everything," he confessed in the most passive way he could.

"During our last session we discussed some things you could do to work on your depression," I reminded him. "Were you able to do them?"

"No, I wasn't," he replied with little concern in his voice.

I kept pressing. "Any idea why?"

"I just didn't get around to them," he answered, as if to imply that it was no big deal.

"Dan, it seems to me that your lack of interest in doing the homework we discussed is a small example of the main theme of your life."

"What do you mean?" he asked, sounding hurt.

"You came here for counseling, and I promised to try to help you. But you won't do the homework in between sessions. You're making it impossible to achieve any improvement. At work, you see yourself falling behind, yet you do nothing to get caught up. In your marriage, your wife nags you constantly about things that need to be attended to, but you keep turning a deaf ear to her. My guess is that you are pretty angry underneath all this passivity. Maybe it's your way of telling people to get off your back."

"Maybe you're right," he said, pacifying me.

"See! There it is again," I insisted.

"Wh-what?"

"I asked you to entertain the idea that your passivity is actually a smoke screen for anger and you passively ignored looking at that by saying, 'Maybe you're right.' "

"So what do you want me to do?" asked Dan. I detected some anger in his voice, which meant we were beginning to get somewhere.

"I want you to come to counseling with more than 'I guess' and 'I don't know' as your replies for everything," I responded. "I want you to make some effort in the direction of getting better rather than just sitting there with that 'Psychologist, heal me' look I get from you."

"I . . . I'm doing the best I can," he defended himself.

"No, you're not. You know that and I know it. You aren't really trying in any area of your life, and that's why you're failing in your job, your marriage, and even in our counseling," I asserted firmly, fearing that I was being too rough in confronting him.

"You don't understand. It isn't that easy!" he continued in his defense.

"I'm not saying it's easy. Getting better is anything but easy. But you aren't putting much of anything into it," I told him frankly.

"I know it. I do that all the time and I hate myself for it," he responded, trying the "kick me" strategy that he often used with his wife and with his boss.

"It sounds like you are wanting me to take pity on you as you beat yourself up for avoiding your problems."

"I feel like a loser who will never amount to anything," he replied, still wanting me to pity him.

"Dan, you aren't a loser, but you are losing. By avoiding the pain of dealing with your problems head-on, you've made them worse. That doesn't warrant sympathy or pity. It warrants trying to understand why and hard work on your part to fight through it," I explained.

"It sounds like you're disgusted with me," he said.

"I'm really not feeling disgusted with you. However I *am* feeling frustrated with your style of wanting good things out of life without wanting to put any effort into getting them. I care enough about you to push on that. I want you to get better, but I don't know how you can if you don't take more responsibility for facing your problems, even when they hurt," I answered.

"I get the point," Dan said. "I've heard it before from my wife, the boss, my parents—from everyone really."

"I know you've heard it before. But that doesn't make it any less true," I responded, hoping he would take this lifelong message and finally do something with it.

"I'll consider what you have to say," he said, as if doing me a favor.

"I hope you will do more than 'consider' what I've said. I'm suggesting you need to act on what I've said. There is a huge difference," I replied.

"You're pushing me where I don't like to be pushed—into actions I really don't want to take. But I know I need to get going."

"I will try to do all I can to help you, Dan, but, yes, the real effort needed has to come from you."

IT TAKES SOME PAINFUL EFFORT

Dan isn't all that different from the rest of us. He wants the nice rewards of a healthy life, but he doesn't want to work hard to do what it takes to get them. I can identify with that. I'm sure you can, too, at least to some extent. The truth that gaining maturity and improvement requires effort and hard work is not new. It's one of those "been around for a long time" truths that I think we need to come back to. The desire to avoid pain and seek pleasure is something we all feel, but it runs counter to emotional health.

I am reminded of that television commercial from

some years ago in which some high school buddies were talking about how easy everything seemed to come for a friend of theirs. As they made these statements, the camera switched to this friend studying late into the night, doing pull-ups at the gym, and closing down a pizza place late at night. I liked that commercial because I think its message was honest. Often the people who look like they have it easy had to work hard for what they have.

If we want it "easy," we have to work hard. If we want a quiz to be easy, we have to study hard. If we want a couple of hours on the tennis court to be easy, we have to train hard. If we want our marriages to be easy, we have to work diligently on making them strong. If we want life to be easy, we have to put our all into it, painfully so. There is no gain without pain. Don't let anyone tell you otherwise. If someone does, that person is lying to you. In a sense, that person is trying to sell you "psychosurgery."

MENTAL IMAGING

As I noted at the beginning of this chapter, there is no such thing as psychosurgery. That does not mean, however, that you cannot do some exercises to help improve your mental outlook on things. One procedure I often recommend to my patients is something called mental imaging.

In this exercise, you create mental images of what your life would be like if you practiced the truth.

Let's say you struggle with the truth "You are not entitled." I want you to imagine that you go to some trouble to hold a door open for someone and they don't say thank you as they walk on by. Imagine that instead of getting angry you are able to stay calm because you realize that you aren't owed a thank you for any kindness you do for others and that you held open the door simply because it was the kind thing to do.

Or imagine you help a friend move to a new house and they don't offer you any refreshments all day or follow through on the promise of a nice meal at the end of the day when everything is finally moved. Instead of decking the person, I want you to imagine feeling good that you helped them move and that courtesy on their part was not something you were owed. Imagine yourself leaving their house feeling satisfied that you performed a helpful service and that that alone is the reward that no one can keep you from enjoying.

Let's say you struggle with the truth "To err is human." I want you to imagine knocking over a stack of canned goods at the grocery store and being able to chuckle about it as you restack them. Or imagine that you get a letter back from the post office because you forgot to put a stamp on it when you originally mailed it. See yourself with a slight grin as you realize your mistake.

On a more serious note, imagine yourself not paying attention while driving and rear-ending the person in front of you, who has slowed down in traffic. Everyone is fine, but both car bumpers are pretty smashed. Imagine yourself getting out of your car to inspect the damage, not in a self-deprecating frame of mind but with a more accepting "Boy, I sure messed this up, didn't I" mind-set. Visualize yourself apologizing, exchanging insurance information and phone numbers, and driving off with an appropriate level of frustration. Imagine telling yourself, as you drive off, that you made a mistake that will be costly but that rear-ending somebody isn't catastrophic and does not need to become a springboard to putting yourself down or getting depressed.

Without being morbid, let's say you have difficulty facing the truth "You are going to die." You "academically" know that you will die some day, but it seems so far in the future it isn't real to you. Imagine you are eating out with family or friends and you suddenly feel a sharp pain shoot across your chest. You can't breathe as you fall on the floor. People try to help you but nothing helps. They call an ambulance, but you die of congestive heart failure in transit to the hospital.

Imagine lying in your casket at the funeral home as mourners walk by to pay their last respects. Imagine your spouse or closest friend going to your place of employment to clean out your office so that someone else can move in to it. Imagine your children (if you have any) having a discussion about you—saying what they remember about you as they grew up, what they will miss, and what they wish you had done with them but didn't. Imagine what you wish you had done with your life that you never got around to doing.

Finally, let's say that you really struggle with the truth, "You can't please everyone." All your life you have been a "people pleaser" and you always feel upset when others don't like you or are displeased with you in some way. Imagine making a phone call to a close friend to tell them that you would like the money back that you lent them months ago. Imagine being in a conversation with people at work and sharing an opinion on a controversial issue that is different from everyone else's. Imagine saying "no" to a friend's request that he/she be able to come see you on a weekend you already had planned to spend with others.

These are just some of the ways that you can use your mind to create mental images of situations in which truth can be more seriously and earnestly practiced. One word of caution: Please do not use mental images that fly in the face of truth or don't involve the practice of truth. For example, please don't imagine yourself never making a mistake, or making a serious mistake and just laughing about it. Don't imagine yourself breaking the world record in the 100-meter dash if your best time ever could have been timed using a calendar! Don't imagine yelling at someone in a department store in an effort to get your way and feeling good about it because they gave in. Mental imaging can be used for constructive growth as a person, but it can also be used for ill. Think through the images you choose, making sure they are reality-based and deepen the truth in you. Give your mind mental images of situations where you are telling yourself the truth and acting in line with it. Give your mind time to "chew" on these images. The more opportunity you have to think on the truth, the healthier you will become.

CHAPTER 10

■

Your Childhood Isn't Over

Experience has taught us that we have only one enduring weapon in our struggle against mental illness: the emotional discovery and emotional acceptance of the truth in the individual and unique history of our childhood.

—Alice Miller

A fair number of people see the past as something that is over and done. It needs to be forgotten and left behind. Yet it isn't quite that easy, is it? As much as it may seem like a self-indulgent waste of time to look backward in time, our unique personal history often demands to be examined and dealt with before life in the here-and-now can fully be lived.

Let me give you a thumbnail sketch of what most self-help books are saying about the importance of our early childhood experiences. These books suggest to us that we begin life with normal needs for love, attention, and affirmation. These are all normal, age-appropriate needs that, for a time, make us want to be the center of the universe. If these needs are adequately met, the theory goes that we can move into adulthood able to let go of these "center of attention" needs and live life as healthy, functioning adults who can both give and take. However, if these needs are not properly met, the belief is that we will carry them into adulthood, with a great deal of hurt, anger, and shame attached to them, and be dysfunctional adults.

Furthermore, these books suggest that many of us, to some degree or another, received inadequate care from our parents and, thus, were emotionally damaged during our childhood. This damage can range from mild to severe, depending on how poorly our fathers and mothers nurtured us. The damage may have resulted from our parents' being indifferent toward us, or from their controlling us too much, or from their trying to live out their need for attention and success through us. In extreme cases damage is caused to us by parents who sexually, verbally, physically, and/or emotionally abused us.

SUPPRESSING THE SELF

Destructive childhood rearing leaves a child feeling he is not accepted and believing his own feelings and uniqueness are not "okay." A child who doesn't feel accepted will develop a "false self" as a protective device. This false self may take the form of a "pleaser," "a straight-A student," "a class clown," or any number of other "masks" that keep the "true self" confined. If not helped to confront this problem, the child moves into adulthood with some kind of mask on and the real person is hidden away. As adults, "masked" people can be quite successful in the world's eyes yet feel tremendous loneliness, depression, emptiness, guilt, shame, and anxiety on the inside.

Robert Young was one of Hollywood's most loved

leading men for more than sixty years. During the 1940s he played the role of the dad in all of the "Mr. Belvedere" movies co-starring Clifton Webb. During the 1950s he had the starring role in the hit television series "Father Knows Best," featured again as the fun-loving and dependable dad (good old Jim Anderson). During the 1960s he portrayed everyone's favorite family physician "Marcus Welby, M.D."

To look at Robert Young you would have thought that here was one man who was secure, rational, and very much at peace with himself. Yet, on January 26, 1991, Robert Young, at age 83, went into his garage, ran a hose from the exhaust pipe of his car to the car window, and tried to commit suicide. He was discovered by chance and rushed to a hospital. He survived, but he was only released from the hospital after he agreed to seek psychiatric help. Upon leaving the hospital, Robert Young told reporters that during his life he had been an alcoholic and had struggled with manic depression. Although he looked happy and normal on the movie and television screens, he was totally miserable in real life.

Robert Young hid behind the masks of his film characters. He is but one of many people who are displaying a confident false self on the outside, while dying emotionally on the inside.

Books written about the "inner child" also tell us that once a child's true self is damaged by his parents, he will spend his adult years looking for a "parent" to take him seriously and to bring him back to health. This need for a "parent" is believed to be largely unconscious and can manifest itself in a variety of ways, like a person's wanting the boss at work to be a father figure or expecting the spouse to meet one's every need.

The implication of these views on early childhood is that each person must come to grips with what happened to him or her in childhood and understand why it happened. If a person faces the truth about his or her childhood, no matter how painful that may be, the belief is that the inner damage can be healed and true adulthood can then be attained.

For example, if a woman can honestly face the fact that her parents did not really love her because the parents were incapable of loving (because of their own emotional damage), the woman can then move toward resolving her feelings of shame and anger. She can begin to understand that she wasn't the reason the love wasn't there. She can quit agonizing over it and quit blaming herself for something she couldn't control. She can even forgive her parents rather than harbor the deep feelings of bitterness and resentment that will only damage her current life. As Dale Carnegie once put it, "Our hate is not hurting them at all, but it is turning our days and nights into hellish turmoil."

From what I see, many of us are "adult children" who are carrying around tremendous hurt, disappointment, and anger from the past. Symptoms like depression, eating disorders, drug and alcohol problems, rage outbursts, anxiety and stress problems, drivenness, even failed marriages are often evidences that the past is still alive in us. Until we deal with the truth about our past, we will continue to run the very real risk of remaining adult children, hiding behind our masks, being chronologically old enough to be called adults but feeling like children inside.

A CHILDHOOD REVISITED

You may feel emotionally immature yourself or you may work or socialize with people who strike you as being emotionally much less mature than their age would suggest. Let me tell you about a patient of mine who was like this and show you just how important it was for her to face the past in order to become a more complete adult and to enjoy her life more fully.

Carol was a newlywed who found she could not enjoy a normal sex life. She wanted to find out why. She came to my office, and after a few moments of introductory conversation, I asked her how I might be of help to her.

"Well, I got married six months ago," she began slowly. "My husband, Mike, is a great guy. I really feel lucky to have him. I know he loves me, and in my heart I know I love him very much too. But in spite of that, we have this problem."

"What sort of problem?" I asked.

"Sex," she answered, saying no more.

"Can you be a little more specific?"

Carol looked down at her hands, avoiding my eyes.

"Well, it's kind of embarrassing for me to talk about this," she said. "The fact is, I just don't want to have sex with my husband. The very thought of sex makes me uncomfortable. Mike gets frustrated because he enjoys sex and wants to have it more frequently than I do."

"So your uneasiness about sex and Mike's desire to have it more often are creating some tension in your marriage, is that correct?" I asked.

She nodded, still not looking up.

"Yes. Mike said I should get some counseling to see why I'm so uptight about sex," she explained.

"Can you think of any reason why having sex with Mike seems to create so much anxiety for you?" I asked.

"Not really. No."

"Sometimes the issues we struggle with in the present are related to incidents in our past," I told her. "Do you think there is any connection between your current anxiety about sex and your upbringing?"

"I don't think so," she replied, not sounding very convincing. "My upbringing was okay."

I asked a variety of other questions and found out that Carol's family physician had said she was in good health. Mike was never abusive toward her, and she didn't seem to have any abnormal pressure being put on her at work or from other sources. Nevertheless, she could not overcome her distaste for sex.

Carol and I spent the next seven counseling sessions discussing her anxiety about sex. We weren't making much progress. Then one session there was a breakthrough.

"I've been extremely nervous this week," Carol stated, almost out of breath.

"Please tell me more," I encouraged her.

"I had a dream last weekend that was very upsetting."

"What happened in the dream?" I asked.

"In the dream an older man and I were playing in my room when I was very young, maybe nine or ten. He suggested we play 'doctor.' I didn't want to, but he kept pressuring me," she said.

"Then what happened?" I prodded.

"The dream ended and I suddenly snapped wide

awake," she replied. "But what was odd was that I had this feeling that it was good that I woke up because I had just escaped something bad happening to me. That seemed ridiculous at the time, but that same feeling stayed with me for several days after that."

"What do you make of that dream?" I asked.

"I don't want to make anything of it," she stated curtly.

"But you sound frightened. That dream scared you, didn't it? It still has you scared."

"Yes, it does. In fact, I'd like to stop talking about it just now, if that's all right. Can we talk about something else?"

"Carol, I get the impression that your dream was trying to tell you something important about your past. I know you're afraid to look at it, but I think there is an important connection between the dream and the anxiety you feel about sex with your husband," I said.

"Maybe so," she responded, not wanting to go further, "but I'd rather not talk about it, please. Not now, anyway."

I didn't pressure Carol to face something she wasn't ready for yet. During our next four sessions she talked about her hopes for the future. She also talked about her friends at work, the people in her apartment complex, and the meals she was learning to cook for Mike. Everything seemed rather routine until one day she arrived at the clinic, her face pale and taut.

When I greeted her in the waiting room, I could see that Carol was upset. She hurriedly walked ahead of me to my office. I found myself having to walk pretty fast just to keep up.

"Carol, you seem pretty upset. What's going on?" I asked.

"I had another dream," she said. "This time it was worse."

"What was the dream about?"

"It was that scene with the older man and me again. We were in my room, like before, and he wanted to play doctor. He wouldn't take no for an answer and he forced me to do some things. He wouldn't quit. I screamed, but no one came to help me."

She related all this in a flat monotone.

"What did you feel like in the dream?" I asked.

"Frightened. Helpless to stop him. He was so much bigger than me. Afraid he'd be angry at me if anyone found out. Afraid of him wanting to do it again," she continued, still with no emotion.

"Carol, I know the dream scares you. Whatever happened to you in the dream was horrifying. Do you think this may have *really* happened to you when you were younger?" I asked, knowing the enormity of the question.

"I can't bring myself to believe it! I just can't believe someone would do that to me. In my dream he removes my clothes and touches me in all my private places. Then he . . . he even has sex with me," she confessed as she began to cry.

"I know that's a frightening thought," I said. "It would be for anyone. It's so frightening, you have repressed it. When Mike approached you for sex, it seems to have triggered a lot of painful memories you weren't aware of from your childhood."

"But I love Mike. I really do," said Carol.

"I believe you," I assured her. "But this incident

from your childhood is hindering your desire to be your husband's sexual partner. We need to talk about what happened to you when you were young."

"But how . . . how could anyone have . . . ?"

"That's one of the things we'll need to talk about," I said. "It won't be easy, but you owe it to yourself and to Mike to face this painful incident and get it behind you."

Carol removed a tissue from her purse and dabbed her eyes.

"I know I need to," she said. "But I'm scared to death. I'm afraid of what I might find out. I'm afraid it will hurt too much. I'm afraid I won't be able to handle it."

"Your fears are understandable. It's frightening to face this kind of issue. I want you to know I believe you can do it and that you will grow a great deal if you will make the effort," I said encouraging her.

"Okay, I'll try," she said, "but I'll still probably try to resist it at times."

"That's fine," I said. "I'll do all I can to help you keep on track."

THE NIGHTMARE OF CHILDHOOD

Carol's dreams were, in fact, trying to tell her something—something horrible enough that she unconsciously resisted seeing it. As we kept talking about her childhood, we came to see that she had been a victim of incest by her father on numerous occasions during those years. We were able to piece together what had happened to her and how it had impacted her self-image, her feelings about sex, and her general mistrust in people as a young child.

We came to see that Carol had learned early in life to view sex as something frightening, something to be feared rather than to be enjoyed. She also learned not to trust men and to see them as users. She carried around tremendous guilt about what had happened, feeling she should have prevented the incest. She also harbored tremendously strong feelings of anger toward her mother for not seeing what was going on and toward her father for what he did. She never told anyone about it because she buried all this so deeply in her memory even she couldn't find it. That was, until she got married.

As it turned out, Carol's marriage to Mike helped surface the incest. Mike's desire for sex, unbeknownst to him, triggered Carol's memories of her horrible past and renewed her anxiety and guilt about sex. Their struggle with sex in marriage was very much tied to Carol's having been a victim of incest when she was a child. As the truth of this problem surfaced, both of them were better able to cope with their sexual problems rather than fight over them. Mike was able to see that Carol's sexual avoidance of him wasn't because of anything he was doing wrong. Carol was able to view her struggle with sex through more understanding eyes and to work in therapy with me on what had happened to her as a child. She joined an incest recovery group and also a couple's therapy group with Mike.

I am happy to say that Carol has made a lot of progress with her painful past. Her hard work has paid handsome dividends, helping her to be more self-accepting and aware of some of the feelings she typically buried. She now has more energy than before, and she feels as if life has become more enjoyable. Her sex life with Mike has improved also.

Carol's story is not unique. A large percentage of the people who come in for counseling are suffering from similar scars from their past. In some cases, sexual abuse is at the core of my patients' struggles. In many other cases, the abuse experienced as a child may have been emotional *and* physical. Some scars from the past run deep; others less so. But they all are in need of healing.

How about *your* childhood? Is it really over? I doubt it. The chances are that you are still dealing with some hurt from the past that hasn't healed. And chances are that this pain from the past is lessening your enjoyment of life. I agree that the past can be used as a cop-out or rationalization by some people for current irresponsibility and problems. It can also be used to justify a lot of "parent bashing" as an escape from growing up. These are certainly to be avoided. But the impact of our past on our present is real and it demands attention.

I agree with Pearl Buck when she said, "One faces the future with one's past." Your past needs attention. Your childhood isn't over. It may be time for you to go back mentally and emotionally to your childhood so that you can face emotional pain you've been keeping buried. Once you deal with your past, you will be freer to "grow up" and be the healthy person you were meant to be.

DISCOVERING YOURSELF

To assist you in your quest for an emotionally healthy life, I want to recommend a number of books to you.

Each contains important truths that can be of great value to you. Read these books carefully. Make notes. Spend time thinking about the truths that you find in them. There is a lot to learn about who you are and why you react the way you do to people and situations in your life. These books will help you in that learning process.

1. *Love Is a Choice,* Robert Hemfelt, Frank Minirth and Paul Meier (Nashville: Thomas Nelson, 1990).
2. *Inside Out,* Larry Crabb (Colorado Springs: NavPress, 1988).
3. *His Image, My Image,* Josh McDowell (San Bernardino: Here's Life, 1984).
4. *Released from Shame,* Sandra Wilson (Downers Grove, IL: InterVarsity, 1990).
5. *Knowing God,* J. I. Packer (Downer's Grove, IL: InterVarsity, 1973).

CHAPTER 11

■

Emotional Problems Are Good

One often learns more from ten days of agony than from ten years of contentment.

—Merle Shain

Back in chapter 7 we spent time looking at the value of facing our problems directly, whether they involve difficult relationships, finances, or self-destructive habits. We learned that it was the getting involved in the struggle—making the effort—that really counted, not the reward.

Now that you've had time to let that become part of your new way of thinking, I want to take that line of thought to another level. I want to try to convince you that emotional problems are good, that much can be gained from them.

None of us wants to feel emotionally troubled, and we often bemoan the times we are. We bitterly complain when we're depressed or anxious or angry about something life has thrown our way. Rarely, if ever, do we see the beneficial side of emotional struggles. Most of us seem certain there isn't a "good" side to them. But I want to try to convince you that you can actually use emotional problems, though quite painful and uncomfortable, to become a stronger person if you can find the courage to face the problems.

In our home, as in many homes, we have smoke detectors installed in several hallways. I don't know all the ins and outs of how they actually detect smoke; I just know that they do. If there ever were a fire in our home while we were asleep, the smoke detector would sense it and would sound an alarm to let us know. By hearing an alarm, we would have a chance either to put out the fire or get out of the house. Without the smoke detector, a fire could quite possibly start undetected in the house while we were sleeping and spread so that by the time we were aware of it, it would be too late for us to get out of the house unharmed.

We humans have a similar alarm system within our bodies. It is a psychological "smoke detector" which sniffs out mental problems and then sets off an emotional warning alarm. Painful feelings such as guilt, anger, depression, and anxiety are, in a very real sense, warning signals—alarms!—telling us that something is not mentally right inside us. They seek to warn us that something needs attention. If not attended to, painful emotions can turn into more serious psychological problems. They are like a fire in our psychological house that can spread and burn it down.

As such, emotional problems are good. They are the warnings we need in order to make us face internal problems so that they won't develop into more serious problems later.

Unfortunately, many of us hear the emotional alarm going off all the time but we ignore it. We may have feelings of depression for days, months, even years, and yet ignore them and act like everything is fine inside. We may explode with rage at the smallest frustration, yet ignore it, even though we know it's a warning signal that all is not well. We may feel chronically anxious yet act as if it means nothing. The whole time our emotions are trying to tell us something, we may refuse to heed them. For many of us, this means much more damage to our lives than need be if we would just listen more attentively to our emotions.

I find it rather amazing that an inanimate object like an automobile can sometimes appear to have more common sense than a human being. If you purchase a brand new car, you'll find it has several computerized check systems built into it. If your car's oil level gets too low, a red warning light will flash on the dashboard. The same happens when the antifreeze, gasoline, and brake and transmission fluids get low. The car senses a level of danger approaching, so it sends a warning for preventative maintenance to be done. If the warning is heeded, the car's running life is extended many extra miles. If not heeded, the car breaks down prematurely.

The human body uses emotions in a similar way. They send signals that say preventative maintenance is needed: more sleep, a more nutritious diet, a reduction of work-related stress, more physical exercise, and most importantly, improvement in our way of thinking. If we would heed these warnings and care for ourselves as well as we do our cars, we would enjoy life more and live a lot longer.

WHEN THE ALARM GOES OFF

Keith fit the profile of a man who was ignoring his emotional warning signs. He had struggled with overwhelming feelings of anger and shame his whole life, yet he refused to let these feelings warn him that he needed help. So he avoided facing the painful internal issues that were crying out for help and, in the process, destroyed his marriage and lost a loving wife. His anger had become so uncontrollable, his wife felt threatened by his outbursts. For her safety, she finally chose to leave him.

Keith felt quite broken by this. He came for counseling to sort things out.

"I know my anger drove her away, but I just couldn't handle her way of doing things," Keith confessed to me. "It aggravated me to no end!"

"Like what?" I asked.

"I guess the biggest irritation was just how much of a pack rat she was. There were things all over the house all the time. It drove me nuts to come home and see all the different piles of clutter everywhere. Sometimes, I would just explode at her."

"Keith, I get the feeling that these outbursts of anger were a problem long before you ever met or married your wife. Is that true?"

"Yeah, I guess so," he confirmed reluctantly. "I suppose I've had a pretty short temper for as long as I can remember. My brother and sister won't have anything to do with me today because they still are mad about how I used to fly off the handle at them when we were kids."

"Did you ever stop long enough to think about what your fits of anger were telling you?" I asked.

"Telling me? What do you mean by that?"

"Well, it seems to me that emotions are signals to us that something isn't quite right inside. You kept getting the signals, but you ignored them," I explained.

"I've never thought of it that way. My anger didn't seem like a signal though. It was more like a reaction to something that frustrated me."

"Our natural tendency is to see our emotions as a statement about someone else rather than as a statement about ourselves. Does that make sense to you?"

Keith pondered that a moment. Suddenly, he smiled sardonically.

"Sure, it makes sense in one way," he said. "I know that when I'm angry I feel like it's a statement about what a jerk the other person is who I'm angry at. Is that what you mean?"

He looked surprised when I nodded my agreement.

"Yes. You thought your anger was a statement about your wife, for example, when it really was a statement about you," I said. "Your anger was trying to alert you to some problems inside of you. You appear not to have used your emotions in that way, so this just created bigger problems in your life."

"You know, I used to be in the military and I worked with radar. What you're saying kind of relates to how we used a rotating beam to spot enemy planes before they got too close," said Keith. "Without the radar, we would have been destroyed. With it, we could react appropriately and lessen the damage."

"Good analogy," I said. "Emotions—even the smallest levels of them—are often trying to warn us to adjust something inside. In that sense, they are extremely helpful and outright good for us."

"I never thought I would call my anger 'good,' but I can see your point. If I can just use it as a cue rather than always spew it all over the place, I might save myself a lot of trouble," he decided.

"Using your emotions this way is something that can be learned," I encouraged Keith. "You can get much better at it with practice. Right now, you're just learning to view your emotions this way. Getting better at it will come with time and effort."

REVAMPING YOUR LIFE

Keith did begin to see his emotions in a new light, and not just anger but also fear, joy, depression, and sadness. He had an especially tough time acknowledging his sadness and using it as a cue that something important was happening inside of him. Keith had been raised to believe that sadness was a sign of weakness and that he shouldn't feel it at all. Yet he did learn to see that even sadness was a feeling inside of him that was trying to cue him to some important issues that needed to be faced in his life.

Keith learned to pay attention to the type of emotions he was feeling as a way of gauging the stresses and challenges he was dealing with in life. He learned to recognize the signs.

Maury Wills of the Los Angeles Dodgers was one of baseball's greatest players. His specialty was stealing bases. One evening, after Maury had stolen his hundredth base of the season, he was interviewed by a television sports commentator. The interviewer noted that Maury had great physical strength, great agility, and great speed. The interviewer asked Maury

Wills if these were the secrets of being a great base stealer.

"They help," said Maury, "but the real secret is in mastering the art of telegraph detection."

"What's that?" asked the broadcaster.

"I make it a point to study the players on the other team," said Maury. "Every person has a set of special quirks and habits, and I try to pick up on them. Usually, these physical signs will telegraph a message to me about what a player is about to do."

"Telegraph?" asked the announcer.

"Right," said Maury. "For example, there's one pitcher who has the habit of pulling the visor of his cap just before he tries to pick me off base. There's a second baseman who takes two steps sideways as the pitcher goes into his windup if it's going to be a 'pitch out' and a throw down to second base. There are dozens of these sorts of motions and gestures that telegraph messages to me about when it's safe or risky to try to steal a base. If I watch the signs closely enough, I never get tagged out when I try to steal a base."

Just as Maury Wills was alert to "messages" "telegraphed" to him by his opponents, so, too, people like my patient Keith have learned to recognize the emotional warnings telegraphed to them. This helps them to stabilize what otherwise would be a roller coaster life of erratic and irrational behavior.

Another reason emotional problems are good has to do with the simple fact that the pain involved in them often motivates us to change. Change is painful, and most of us would rather not change unless we have to. Painful emotions often serve as the "have to." You know what I am talking about if you have ever been so miserable that you would do almost anything in order to stop hurting. The two great motivators in life seem to be misery and desire. Emotional problems are often the "misery" that motivates us to try to move beyond the status quo.

I see evidence of this truth all the time in the counseling I do. The majority of my patients come for help because their pain level got so bad that they "either had to come in or not make it." This tendency to wait until things are so bad that it becomes "do or die" is unfortunate because a great deal of misery could have been avoided with a more preventative outlook. It is like the person who gains a few pounds but refuses to exercise until those few pounds have turned into twenty or thirty. A small molehill of a problem turns into a huge mountain of one because people do not use the early, smaller levels of pain involved as the motivation to do something.

There is an important medical parallel to what I'm suggesting in this chapter. We have all run into it a number of times. We will on occasion develop a physical symptom, such as a fever, and we'll go to see a physician to find out what is causing it. The misery the fever causes not only alerts us to the fact that something is wrong physically, but it also motivates us to go find out what it is.

Recently, for example, I developed a severe sore throat, one of those kinds where each time you swallow your whole body yells, "Ouch!" Normally, I ignore such painful symptoms, choosing instead to be macho and just tough it out. But in this instance, the pain only became worse. The sore throat was both a cue and motivation to do something. So I went to our family physician and found out I had bronchitis and pharyngitis. He put me on antibiotics and in a few days I was feeling better.

But what if my throat had never become sore nor the pain become severe? I would never have known something was "ill" inside my system. The disease could have become much worse. As much as I moaned and complained about the sore throat, it was actually a blessing. It "blessed" me by saying, "Hey, Thurman, you have a problem and it's going to keep hurting you until you fix it."

In a perfect world you would never have any medical symptoms because there would be no viruses or bacteria. In the real world there are both. Similarly, in an ideal world you would never see clinical depression, phobias, eating disorders, panic attacks, or any other psychological symptoms because there would be no psychological stresses or distorted thinking to help cause them. But in the real world we have a variety of psychological challenges and we do suffer from the emotional symptoms they cause. As strange as it may sound, I am convinced that these emotional symptoms are blessings. They are good news for us. They are just what we need both to be alerted (cued) and motivated (challenged to do something).

There is a great deal of evidence that suggests there is a direct link between our mental/emotional status and our physical well-being. An example of this is found in the life of Kate Jackson, the beautiful dark-haired actress who has starred in such TV shows as "The Rookies," "Charlie's Angels," and "Scarecrow and Mrs. King."

To look at Kate Jackson, you would have always assumed that she had the world on a string. She was successful (three hit TV series); she was pretty (her face had appeared on the covers of dozens of national magazines); she was wealthy (her Beverly Hills mansion cost $2.4 million); and she was famous (her fan mail arrived by the truckloads). Internally, however, she was a bundle of nerves. Emotional signals began to telegraph messages to her, but Kate ignored them. She had flashes of anger; she had days of listlessness; she had bouts with self-doubt.

Although the external emotional signs were warning her that she was in a "danger" mode, she continued to work and drive and push herself beyond her limits. Then one night she had a bizarre experience. Kate had a nightmare in which she dreamed that something was terribly wrong with her physically. The nightmare was even specific enough to make her think that the problem was breast cancer.

"I know it sounds weird," Kate told a *Redbook* magazine reporter (April 1991), "but that's exactly what happened. I believe your body talks to you, and you *have* to listen to it!"

Kate went to a clinic and had a mammogram. Sure enough, there was a malignant growth in her left breast. It was removed by surgery in 1987. This caused Kate to re-evaluate her life. She began to try to get more sleep and to work less, but the demands of a hit TV show continued to pull at her. Soon, she was back into the same ultra-stressful lifestyle she had been in prior to the surgery. Then in September 1989, the cancer appeared again in the left breast. To correct it Kate had to undergo a partial mastectomy and reconstructive plastic surgery.

"I was scared," she said of that time. "I was petrified. I thought, 'Why me?' I was angry."

It took the second bout with cancer to convince

Kate Jackson that ignoring her emotional signals had been a bad decision. She set about immediately to correct matters. She sold her posh California home and moved to a serene 125-acre farm in Virginia. She began a daily program of physical exercise. She changed her diet to fruit, grains, fish, and cereal—no fats, no junk food, no cigarettes. She also started getting plenty of sleep at night.

"I don't want the anxiety I used to live with," says Kate. "That's why I moved to Virginia. I don't want the stress. I don't need all that."

We all can't afford to care for ourselves the way Kate Jackson did, but we can afford to learn Kate Jackson's lesson. The next time you are tempted to view your emotional struggles as bad, you might think about seeing them as your mind's way of telling you that it wants to keep you healthy. It's warning you that something inside you is working against that. To think otherwise is to miss the signal.

SEEKING THE TRUTH

Having read this chapter, I want you to use the truth you learned herein to initiate a new self-examination exercise. The procedure is simple to follow, yet its results will be profound.

I want you to find a time and place when you can be alone with a pad of paper and a pencil or pen. Across the top of the paper I want you to write "Emotional problems are good." In a column on the left side, I want you to number down the page from one through ten.

Now, sit and meditate for half an hour on that statement. Think about the specific emotional problems you are now coping with. Consider the reasons these problems are good: what are they alerting you to and making you aware of? Write your responses. Try to come up with ten. Don't be in a hurry. Take all the time you need. You may want to do this same exercise during your quiet time for several days.

You can enhance this procedure by reading back through your TRUTH journal entries and meditating on the other truths you have learned in this book, such as "The virtue lies in the struggle, not the prize" or "To err is human." As you compile your response lists, keep them in your journal. Have them handy to refer to the next time you find yourself going through an emotional struggle. They will remind you that emotional problems are good.

CHAPTER 12

∎

Life Is Difficult

> Life is like playing a violin
> solo in public and learning the
> instrument as one goes on.
> —Edward Bulwer-Lytton

Does the name Vinko Bogataj ring a bell? No? Well, let me give you some hints about who this very famous person is. He drives a forklift in a factory that manufactures anchor chains. He lives a quiet life with his wife, two daughters, and mother-in-law. In his spare time, he paints and carves wood.

Any guesses yet? None? Well, let me give you a couple more hints. Vinko Bogataj lives in Lesce, Yugoslavia, and is probably the most famous retired ski jumper in history. Still no guesses?

Well, even if you don't recognize his name, you've probably seen Vinko Bogataj. You see, Vinko happens to be the poor "agony of defeat" guy of ABC's "Wide World of Sports" fame. He was the one who took an incredible head-over-heels fall while in a ski jump competition in Oberstdorf, Germany, in 1971. Unfortunately for Vinko, "Wide World of Sports" was there to capture every inglorious second of his spectacular fall. They have been broadcasting Vinko's fall at the

opening of their show every week for years, perma-
nently immortalizing him in the "Sports Hall of
Shame." Jim McKay, the voice of "Wide World of
Sports" for the thirty years it has been on the air, says
that perhaps the single most-asked question about the
show concerns this poor skier from Lesce.

I don't know about you, but I kind of understand
how Vinko must have felt when he messed up for all
the world to see. In my own not-so-glorious ways
throughout my life, I have made some pretty spectacular falls. While mine weren't there for the whole
world to see as was Vinko's, I still felt like I had about
the same amount of embarrassment and shame that
went along with them. Hardly anything feels worse
than these moments.

I remember one of those moments as if it were yesterday. I was in Michigan giving one of my "Thinking
Straight" seminars before an audience of about three
hundred people. I was covering some important ma-
terial using an overhead projector. Thinking I was
writing on a transparency, I actually wrote all over
the clear glass plate that light is projected through
instead. I can't tell you how humiliated I felt when I
realized my mistake. There I was in front of three
hundred people staring at an overhead projector with
my scribblings all over the glass plate and no way to
erase them. If there had been an exit door nearby, I
would have slithered out as quickly as possible and
never returned to the beautiful state of Michigan
again. I felt like Vinko Bogataj sailing off the side of
the ski jump. Talk about feeling like you have been
walking around in public with toilet paper hanging
out of your pants! Fortunately, the people in atten-
dance found this extremely funny, and a member of

the audience went and got me some wet paper towels to clean off the glass plate so I could continue the seminar.

Maybe you have had a Vinko Bogataj moment or two in your life. Maybe you have found yourself gliding down the ski jump of life ready to take glorious flight, thinking to yourself, *What a piece of cake!* only to lose your balance and go careening off in some disastrous direction. As you lay there emotionally bruised and bleeding from your mistake, you probably felt the complete loss of self-worth and confidence that goes with moments like these. You might also have felt the cold stare of those who were there to observe that not-so-grand moment in your life.

Why all this fuss about our friend Vinko and his famous fall off some ski jump in Germany? Well, I want to use his experience, and our own like it, to suggest another critically important truth that we need to fully understand as we head down the ski jump that each day represents: Life is difficult. Vinko found that out as he tried to keep his balance as an athlete. We find this out each day as we try to keep our balance as humans.

Most everyone on the planet seems to have a personal "Life is difficult" story to tell. These stories are sometimes amusing, sometimes heartbreaking, often somewhere in between. But listen closely to how these stories are told. You'll notice that the storytellers are often surprised, even insulted that life had proven to be difficult. It is as if they had been operating under the assumption that life should be easy and smooth. They often tell their stories with great resentment and anger as if life had chosen only them to inflict misery on. In a very real sense, they have not come to grips with the great truth that life is difficult. Instead, they are still living in some childlike world where life is all "peaches and cream" and every challenge is easily navigated.

A number of years ago, I started to realize that I was one of those people. My realization began when I read Dr. M. Scott Peck's book *The Road Less Traveled*. He opens the book with the simple statement, "Life is difficult," and proceeds to call it one of the greatest truths and one that few people come to grips with. I remember thinking I had wasted my $7.95 on the book if that was all it had to say to me. "Tell me something new!" was my initial (and arrogant) thought.

As I thought more about what Dr. Peck was trying to say, though, I could see he was hitting closer to home than I cared to see. As much as it hurt to admit it, I realized I hadn't really come to grips with this truth. I saw more deeply than ever before that I had spent all of my life believing that life should be easy and that something was horribly wrong when difficulty dared to show up. I saw how much I resented difficulty and how I responded to it with a "How dare you do this to me!" attitude. I often found myself whining and moaning whenever difficulty came my way.

Essentially, I had not grown up! I was looking at life much as a child does—through rose-colored glasses that made life look prettier and easier than it really is. When life wasn't pretty or easy, I would throw an internal, and sometimes external, temper tantrum that would match any five year old's best. Sound familiar? Maybe you can identify with my own struggle to accept that life is, indeed, difficult. Maybe you also want to keep seeing life in rosier shades than it really is. Maybe you, like me, do your fair share of whining and moaning when life is tough. If so, I don't think we are alone.

Dr. Peck explains in *The Road Less Traveled* why he believes life is difficult. I found his argument compelling. He believes that the process of confronting and solving problems is an inherently painful one, and since life poses an endless series of problems, life is always difficult. Dr. Peck goes on to suggest that four tools are critically important in facing painful problems head-on: delay of gratification, balance, acceptance of responsibility, and dedication to truth. I agree that all four tools are required in confronting life's difficulties, but I'm convinced it is the last tool, dedication to truth, that is the most important of all. I will more clearly state why in the last chapter of the book.

With the evidence all around us that life is difficult, I am amazed at how many of us still refuse to accept this truth. Believe me, the typical person I counsel appears to believe that life should be easy and often blows a gasket when life proves otherwise. Let me give you an example.

Becky came to counseling with enough anger and bitterness to fill an ocean. She often lost her temper and finally came to counseling because her boss told her that either she go to counseling or she go out the company door. She wasn't exactly what you might call a "happy to be here" kind of patient. The following exchange took place during one of our sessions.

"I don't know why I'm here," Becky grunted. "My boss pretty much forced me to come because I lost my cool a few times with some customers at work."

"So you are not really sure you need to be here?"

"I'm sure I don't need to be here!" she adamantly replied. "I may lose my temper every so often, but the people I get angry at usually deserve it. They put me through so much unnecessary hassle I just can't help but get furious with them!"

"You don't feel you have much control over your anger at those times."

"It feels like a wave coming over me. I can't stop it. I speak before I think and end up getting myself in trouble," she stated as if she were confessing to a priest.

"Becky, I believe it's just the opposite. I believe you think *before* you speak. Play along with that thought for a minute. Let's assume you think before you speak. What do you think you might be telling yourself prior to getting angry at these people?"

"Your guess is as good as mine," she answered as if I were one of her customers hassling her, not wanting to be much help.

"Come on, give it a try. What do you think is going through your mind about these people who put you through so much unnecessary hassle?"

"That they are jerks and shouldn't be making my life so difficult!"

"So you think they are making your life more difficult than it should be, is that it?"

"Yes. I don't need them to make my life any more difficult than it already is."

"Becky, let me ask you what may seem like an insane question. How difficult do you think your life should be?"

"What do you mean?"

"Well, you said that these customers make your life more difficult than it should be. That seems to imply that you have some sense of how difficult life ought to be. So let me ask you again, how difficult should your life be?''

''I don't think my life ought to be *that* difficult! I shouldn't have to put up with people who have nothing better to do than irritate me!''

''Well, let me ask you an equally insane question. Why not?''

''What do you mean, 'Why not'? Why should anyone have to put up with people like that?''

''Because life is full of people like that.''

''What? You gotta be kidding me. I'm supposed to accept that life is full of jerks like that?''

''Yes.''

''Dr. Thurman, with all due respect, I can't believe you're saying that to me. Why would I want to accept that?''

''Look at the price you are paying for not accepting it! You walk around ready to explode at a moment's notice, and you are close to losing a job you told me you like pretty much. The price you are paying for thinking life ought to be easy and 'jerk free' is already pretty high and could go even higher if you lose your job.''

''I just can't accept that my job should have hassles in it like that!'' she fought back, refusing to budge.

''Becky, let me play a little rougher with you. Why do you think your life should be any different from anyone else's? Why should you have the only job on the planet where you don't have to deal with less than wonderful people? Are you royalty? Do you deserve a hassle-free life and the rest of us don't?''

''No, I don't think anyone should have to put up with difficulties that aren't necessary.''

"Well, that doesn't really solve the problem, does it? Whether any of us *should* have to put up with irritating or unnecessary problems or not, they show up on our doorstep anyway. There are lots of difficulties in life, some necessary and some that don't really have to happen, but they do happen. You seem to be saying that rather than face that and accept it you are just going to stay mad at it, no matter how much you lose in the process."

"When you put it that way, it doesn't really sound too good," she sheepishly responded.

"Maybe the truth of the matter is that that attitude *isn't* too good. Maybe that attitude is keeping you from handling life more maturely than you do."

"I don't know. Maybe you are right," she conceded without really sounding convinced.

"Becky, let me be bold with you. I *am* right on this. You are telling yourself that your life ought to be free from certain kinds of difficulties, and you get furious when it isn't. The truth is that your life is just like mine and everyone else's—it has difficulties in it that aren't a lot of fun to deal with. And these difficulties are, in a sense, testing how mature you are. Your boss is trying to tell you that you are not doing too well on the 'maturity test' at work and that you need to do better or you will lose your job. For you to do better, you are going to need to come more fully to grips with the truth that life is difficult, both in tolerable and not so tolerable ways, whether we like it or not. We can choose to squeal like stuck pigs when life is difficult or do the mature thing and accept the difficulty and handle it as best we can."

"I think I'm getting your point. You're saying my anger toward the customers is tied to immaturely believing that they shouldn't be making my life difficult when the truth of the matter is that life *is* difficult and they are just proving that to me. I'm at odds with the fact that life is difficult rather than accepting it and dealing with it."

"That is exactly what I am trying to get across."

"I gotta tell you that your being right about this isn't much comfort. I still don't think I will be able to handle jerks at work any better. I will still tend to speak before I think."

"Isn't that why you are in counseling? Aren't you here to work on that problem? Don't you think your boss will keep you as long as you work on the problem and show some improvement over time?"

"Yes, she will keep me if I get better. She likes my work in general, and she seems pretty invested in helping me mature as a worker. And now that you mention it, maybe I am in counseling because I need to handle people better than I do. And not just at work but in my personal life as well. I get pretty angry there also."

"Becky, a lot of different issues figure in to your anger outbursts at work, and we can use our sessions to explore what they are. So far, I am just suggesting that one of the more core issues is a basic unwillingness to accept the truth that life is difficult. Your work life was just pointing that out to you through the 'jerks' you were being asked to help. Life is a pretty good teacher at times if we will let it be. In this case, it was trying to teach you that you hadn't learned an important truth that you need to learn to have a successful life. I'm confident you can learn to deeply accept that life is difficult and not be so at odds with it."

"I sure hope so. I don't want to spend the rest of

my life blowing up at people and things that bother me."

My sessions with Becky often came back to the "Life is difficult" truth. Time and time again, she would bring into my office complaints about this hassle and that hassle, angry and resentful that life had dared to be difficult again. We kept trying to look at what life was telling her and kept trying to break past her unwillingness to listen. She did make progress, though it was slow at times. Bit by bit, she started to accept that life is inherently difficult and that staying at odds with that truth was only hurting her.

When I began writing this chapter, I was tempted to take the "Life is difficult" truth and give you some more dramatic versions of it to prove the point. I was tempted to relate patient stories like that of a patient of mine who was chased around her house as a child by a parent with a knife in his hand threatening to kill her, or that of a patient of mine who was forced by her father to have sex when the mother was out of the house, or that of my patient who lost all of his hard-earned money and a business he had devoted his life to because his business partner swindled money from the company and put it in bankruptcy. These are the stories that break your heart. Instead, I opted for one that involved a patient facing the difficulty of dealing with "jerks" at work.

The point is this: Whether in small ways or large ways or in-between ways, life is difficult. That is a great truth. Stepping out on the planet believing otherwise is to invite emotional trouble on a scale that none of us can ultimately survive. Becky came to see that. I hope you already have. If not, I hope this chapter has helped remind you of it.

CHAPTER 13

∎

You Reap What You Sow

Who is man's chief enemy?
Each man is his own.
—Anacharsis

More than a few of us spend a lot of time hoping, often at some unconscious level, that this last truth, "You reap what you sow," isn't true. But, true it is.

We eat a large bowl of our favorite ice cream while watching television at night and then hope the scales won't hold us accountable the next morning. We spend money as if there were no tomorrow and hope the charge card people will forget to bill us at the end of the month. We don't exercise, yet we expect our bodies to remain healthy and firm throughout our lives. We ignore our kids and hope they will grow up to be mature adults. We race down the highway at break-neck speed and hope there will be no police officers around.

In dozens of different ways we act and hope that we can avoid the consequences that almost always accompany those actions.

The sad truth is that sometimes we do *seem* to get away with certain actions and it doesn't appear that we are reaping in accordance to what we have sown. People often speed without getting caught by the police. People sometimes cheat on their taxes and don't get audited by the IRS. Some people even commit murder and are not caught and made to go to prison. Many other examples would come to mind, I'm sure, if you were to give it a moment of thought.

So it appears that people can escape restitution at times, that they can beat their fate, that they can fool themselves and others if they are just crafty enough. Yes, it *seems* that way. But I believe we *always* reap what we sow, even if it doesn't appear that way. Everything we do contributes to who we are. Every action we take adds another stitch to the fabric of our character. We never actually get away with anything because whatever we do leaves its impression on our memories, our conscience, our very soul.

Take the highway speeder. He may, in fact, speed down the interstate at 90 miles per hour and not get a ticket. Yet he has sown something into who he is. His "self"—his personality, his value system, his innate sense of right and wrong—has been affected in a negative and self-degrading way. He has sown another stitch into the part of his "being" that disrespects rules, that rebels against authority, that treats other people's safety with indifference, and that shows a calloused hostility toward society. He may reach his destination that day in record time, much to his own delight, but he will have done so at the expense of his dignity and humanity. Most regrettably of all, he will probably have done all this without even realizing it.

The sowing we do each day in small ways shows up sooner or later in several significant ways. Years may go by before the more noticeable signs show up;

but they do ultimately appear. We may be shocked when we see the final fruits of what we have sown, but that just reflects how naive we have been. Most of us assume that the small, seemingly unimportant things we do each day aren't shaping us. But shape us they do.

When you stop to think about real-life incidents such as the demise of Gary Hart's presidential campaign, Pete Rose's baseball career, Donald Trump's financial empire, Leona Helmsley's hotel wealth, Rock Hudson's movie legacy, Jessica Savitch's news career, Elvis Presley's entertainment impact, and Jim Bakker's religious ministry, I think you can start to understand the point I am making. In each of these cases, these people seemed to be doing fine—even fantastic—on the surface. But in retrospect, we can see clearly the seeds of their downfall were sown all along the way to reach fruition in the banner headlines that shocked us all. Each downfall began with a small, seemingly innocuous action here, an apparently unimportant behavior there. Small seeds of extravagance and carelessness sown along life's way turned into weeds of destruction later on.

I see the "You reap what you sow" truth all the time in the lives of my patients. I am no stranger to this truth myself. Allow me to share an example with you from my life that illustrates the point, and then I want to take you into the life of one of my patients to illustrate the point even further.

When I was in elementary school, I was fascinated by foul words (as many young boys are). When I say "fascinated," I mean that I had a childish curiosity about which words were considered to be foul and why. I was admonished by my parents and my teachers not to use such words, but seeing the reaction that such words could evoke from people when I used them, I remained "fascinated" by their power and impact. As a compromise, when I was upset, I would just *think* one of those cuss words. Eventually, however, their shock value wore off on me, so just to grandstand a little or to draw attention to myself, I would use some foul language around my friends now and then. I got a kick out of their reactions.

By the time I entered high school, as you might well imagine, the problem of swearing had become worse. I found myself more regularly saying foul words to myself whenever the moment seemed to call for one. I was also more casual about swearing in front of others. I was quicker to cuss if I became angry or just wanted to be noticed. As a sports nut, I thought it was the macho thing to cuss on the athletic field, so I did my fair share of it. Sometimes, the other guys and I even had contests to prove our manliness by trying to find out who had the most vulgar mouth.

College was no better, maybe even a little worse. By the time a person reaches college, he often has become even more creative in his range of foul words. And if I was ever lacking for any, my friends were always a ready source of foul words I hadn't even heard before. So my use of off-color language continued, usually just to myself, but to some extent also in front of others.

After college I came to see how detrimental swearing could be to my personal self-esteem, my reputation among my peers, and my role as a husband and father. I made a conscious decision to stop. The problem was, I had allowed the habit of swearing without thinking about it to be programmed into me for more than twenty years. I would often react or respond to a situation by cussing before I even had a chance to control my thoughts or words.

Now, as a man well into his thirties, I find myself still struggling with my effort not to use foul language. More times than I care to admit, I catch myself starting to cuss at situations and people without even realizing it. If angry enough, I even cuss at people directly. I feel like I sometimes cannot control what I say.

Last year I was working out on an exercise machine at the health club where I am a member. A man I had never seen before came up and asked me how much longer I would be using the machine. I said, "At least another fifteen minutes." This angered him, and as he walked off, he called me something unprintable. I was hot, tired, and worn out from the workout, so instinctively I reverted to my old ways and I called him the same thing back. If I had not just as quickly come to my senses about what I'd said and apologized, we might have come to blows. How ridiculous, right? Yet it happened. I'm ashamed of the incident, but it underscored once again that, as an adult, I'm still reaping the bad seed I had sown as a younger man.

Whereas some people don't think cussing is any big deal, I do. I don't think mature adults need to use vulgar words. I don't think mature people need to reach into the gutter in order to find adequate words to express themselves. And I want to be a mature person. So I find myself fighting this problem, this ongoing battle. I can't seem to completely resolve this lingering cussing problem. What began as a seemingly harmless fascination with foul language when I was a child turned into a cussing habit by high school and a problem that has carried over into my present life. I'm better now, but not rid of the habit.

As I said before, I feel embarrassed about my cussing. I feel I will never be as mature a person as I can be until I control my tongue. It takes a lot of hard work to keep the problem in check. And now, as a father, I find myself having to bite my tongue every so often to keep from saying something in front of my kids that would put some words in their minds that I don't want there.

The point is, a lot of things start off harmlessly early on, but then are sown more deeply as we age, and finally become quite entrenched in us. Thus, even if we don't always pay publicly for negative things we have done or bad habits we have developed, we often pay privately through decreased feelings of personal maturity, the loss of self-esteem, and moral degeneration. Further embarrassment and shame may be added when the problem does surface publicly. Let me take you into my counseling office and show you what I mean.

AS THE TWIG IS BENT

Hank came to see me because of a problem he was having with pornography. Specifically, he found himself frequently renting videos with strong sexual content and buying "adult" magazines. He would often do this when his wife was going to be gone from the house all day or for a weekend. Hank's compulsion to rent pornographic videos and to buy lewd magazines was strong, and he felt like he couldn't stop himself from turning to pornography whenever an opportunity arose.

Because of strong religious values, Hank felt a tremendous amount of guilt and shame about his problem with pornography. He kept it hidden from his wife and friends. He experienced a great deal of anxiety about being seen renting or buying the pornography. Even when that went "smoothly," Hank felt "dirty" about doing it. He had lost a great deal of self-respect because of the problem. He came to counseling hoping to find a way out of the struggle. During one of our early sessions, Hank and I traced the origins of his problem.

"Hank, tell me if you can how far back your struggle with pornography goes."

"Well, I remember when I was really young that some of the older kids in our neighborhood had some adult magazines they were showing to everyone," Hank recalled. "I didn't really know what was going on, so I just looked at the pictures too."

"About how old were you at the time?" I asked.

"Somewhere about five or six, not any older I'm sure."

"What else do you remember?" I prodded.

Hank's eyes narrowed and he rubbed his chin. "Uh, we had a neighborhood drugstore that had a magazine rack. A lot of the magazines had provocative pictures on them of scantily clad women. I'd go in there and pretend I was checking out the new sports magazines, but really I was looking at the adult magazines. Sometimes when the clerk was busy with a customer, I'd grab one of the magazines and quickly leaf through the pages and look at all the photographs."

"Anything else?"

"Well, yeah," said Hank, "there was some temptation at home. My father kept a stack of men's magazines in his closet. Whenever my folks would be out of the house for any reason, I'd sneak into their room and look at those magazines. I'd always make sure I put them back exactly the way they were when I found them. I was scared to death that my dad might suspect I'd been looking at them. He never mentioned it, however, so I just figured I had gotten away with something."

"Did this go on a long time?" I asked.

"Oh sure, for years," Hank admitted. "I'd think about those magazines pretty often. When I got older and my folks would go out for a night together, I'd love it. It meant I would be home alone for hours with those magazines. I was pretty obsessed with them even then."

"What age were you?"

"I discovered the magazines when I was about ten," said Hank, "and I kept sneaking into the closet to look at them right on into my teenage years. When I hit puberty, it felt like I had lost my mind over sex. I couldn't seem to think about *anything* except sex. I tried getting involved in sports and that helped a little bit, but once practice or a game was over, my mind would often revert right back to thoughts about sex."

"Did you ever consider talking to your father about this problem you were having?"

Hank flinched. "Whoa! My dad? Are you kidding? My dad never once had a man-to-man talk with me about sex or girls or dating or anything like that. No, neither one of us ever brought up the subject."

"It appears that you and your father had a similar problem with pornography but never disclosed it openly," I replied. "You became a 'chip off the old block' in a sense."

"In later years I picked up on that, but not when I was still a kid," Hank answered. "In those days the guys at school would talk about girls. You know, we'd say things in the locker room to make other guys think we knew a lot about sex. After we got our drivers' licenses, we'd try to get into R-rated or X-rated movies. It seemed like we talked about sex all the time. Most of us had steady girlfriends by then, and we were all into heavy petting. We'd brag a lot, but the fact was, we didn't know as much as we pretended we did."

"What about after high school? Did it continue?"

"Definitely," said Hank. "I went to college and I was in a dorm room with a couple of guys who would buy porno magazines and pass them around. I bought some too. This was back in the days before videos."

"You were of legal age by then, right?"

"Yeah. I could buy anything I wanted. My buddies and I would sometimes go to X-rated films at a sleazy theatre in a town ten miles from the college campus. Back then they still had drive-ins too, and some of them would run double feature R-rated movies on the weekends. I knew I was hooked on this stuff when I couldn't find anyone to go with me one weekend and I drove out to the drive-in by myself."

"That must have been pretty lonely," I suggested.

"Yes, it was," said Hank. "But the sad part about it was I liked to be by myself whenever I looked at pornography. I would fantasize that I was the guy that all those sexy girls were going crazy over. It was exciting, an escape of sorts. It actually helped me feel less lonely at times. At least for a couple of hours."

"Did these fantasies ever spill over into real life?"

"Little by little, they did," Hank admitted. "I'd find myself looking at the girls who were in class with me or who were walking across campus, and I'd carry this secret lust for them. Sometimes when I was on a date with a nice girl, I'd let a suggestive remark come out. It usually didn't go over very well. I even got my face slapped one time. You know, as I look back on that now, I can see how some women get the notion that the only thing men ever think about is sex, sex, sex. With a guy like me, that isn't too far from the truth."

"Once college was over, what was the struggle like?"

"I got a job that brought me here to Texas," Hank explained, "but I didn't know a single person outside of the people at work. My nights were lonely and my weekends were pure torture. So I fell back on the one cure for loneliness and boredom that had always seemed to help before. I started buying adult magazines. Also, there were X-rated videos available for home viewing by then. I'd sometimes spend my whole day at work just marking time until I could go to the video store and rent some more porno flicks. The anticipation was always really strong, but later that night, after I watched the videos, the sense of loneliness would come over me again. I felt empty."

"What about after you met some new people here?" I asked. "Did that help you with your struggle against the pornography?"

"Somewhat. Especially after I met some girls and started going out on dates. That gave me something other than videos and magazines to think about. But it wasn't a cure-all. There still were times when no dates were available and so I'd turn again to the pornography. It became a compulsion I couldn't seem to control, much less overcome."

"Eventually, you got married, though. Did that help?"

Hank lowered his head slightly. "I thought it would, but maybe I expected too much. I mean, my wife and I have an okay sex life and all, but my mind seems filled with zillions of pictures of women I've looked at in magazines and on videos. That's distracting to me and it's unfair to her. I find myself wanting variety, but one woman can't possibly be as versatile as a store filled with a hundred videos. So I find myself turning to the pornography whenever I want variety, and that only compounds the problem. It makes sex with my wife less desirable. I know she must feel that I don't love her and that I don't find her sexually attractive. She tries to talk to me, but I just can't bring myself to tell her what's been going on behind her back."

"You're afraid that she'll be hurt and angry," I said.

"No doubt about it," Hank insisted. "It would shock her and break her heart. She wouldn't be able to understand. I can't imagine ever being able to tell her about my 'hidden' life."

"You're mostly afraid of losing her respect, aren't you? And you also want to protect the positive image she has of you."

"Sure. Every husband wants his wife to respect him. She thinks of me as a highly moral man. I don't want to shatter that view. But it's all a false front. And that's one reason why I've come to you. This is more than I can handle alone. I need some help. Big time help."

"You've taken a positive step," I reassured Hank. "I know your struggle with pornography has been a tough one. But if your love for your wife was strong enough to motivate you to come here for help, you may be a lot closer to fitting the image she has of you than you think."

Hank's face lifted and he smiled ever so slightly. I could tell he felt encouraged and he was glad he had come for counseling.

"The origin of your struggle goes back to when you were very young," I told Hank. "By looking at the pictures in the magazines, you became part of the group of onlookers. You weren't alone. It felt good to be part of the gang.

"Later, when you became old enough to derive sexual stimulation from such pictures, that just added another dimension to your desire to want to make pornography part of your life. You reinforced these feelings so frequently, the habit became very strongly rooted in you. Today, the habit is controlling you rather than you controlling the habit. In the process, your self-esteem and self-respect have taken a real beating."

Hank weighed my words, then nodded his agreement. "Yeah, I think that pretty much hits the nail on the head. So what am I going to do about it?"

"I won't kid you," I said forthrightly. "You have spent so many years entrenched in this problem, it will be a tough one to overcome. I know that isn't exactly what you want to hear, but it's true nevertheless. We all reap what we sow, for better or for worse. In your situation, the sowing of all those thoughts and actions over the years has created strong habits that have become an addiction for you."

Hank contemplated that a moment, then said, "I hadn't thought about my struggle with pornography as the result of reaping what I had sown, but I guess you're right. Every time I purchased a magazine or rented one of those videos, I was sowing more of the problem. Now I'm reaping all the negative results of that. I really wasn't getting away with anything all those years I thought people weren't 'catching' me at the porn shops. If I had really wanted to conquer this problem, I should have been *catching myself*."

"Maybe that's true," I said, "but before you beat yourself up too much, I want to point out that you didn't exactly get a lot of help along the way. Your father, by keeping adult magazines in his closet, was giving tacit approval to pornography. Also, you grew up in a culture that often treats women as sexual playthings, which was another message to you that it was all right to think of women as pornographic objects."

I let that sink in, then added, "There are a number of other elements that figure into the equation here, but you understand what I'm getting at. I agree that you made your own choices along the way and that you are responsible for those choices. But you didn't get much help along the way either."

I spent a few minutes trying to explain the fine line between personal responsibility and impressionability—young boys being influenced by externals, like male role models and cultural attitudes, for example.

"I appreciate what you're trying to say," Hank told me. "I know my dad's attitude toward sex didn't help my situation. And growing up in a country that seems as sex-obsessed as America is probably only fanned the fire. Still, I can't get away from the fact that my choices were really bad."

"You're suffering now from the consequences of your previous choices. I hope you can let that be enough punishment and just channel your efforts into understanding the problem and learning how to fight it."

THE ONGOING STRUGGLE

That is just what Hank has been doing with some success. He's fighting his problem as best he knows how.

We have continued to explore his background and how it has affected his views of women, sex, and love. We also have spent a great deal of time examining how he used and still uses pornography to run from loneliness and boredom. We have further examined how pornography fed his narcissistic need to be in control, to be powerful, and to be the center of attention.

These efforts have helped Hank to see his struggle in a more honest light and have helped him develop more self-control when it comes to buying magazines and renting videos. Hank opened up about his problem to a close friend who was also struggling in this area. Almost like friends involved in Alcoholics Anonymous, Hank and his friend have agreed to discuss their mutual problem regularly and to encourage each other to keep fighting it.

Hank's story is not unlike one that most of us could tell. While his struggle was with pornography, it could have been with any number of other things.

The point I have been making in this chapter is that many of our current problems are simply the long-term or immediate reapings of unhealthy thoughts or actions we have sown. As the quotation opening this chapter suggests, we are often our own worst enemies in that we do sow some pretty bad thoughts and actions in our lives, causing us to later reap some pretty painful and destructive outcomes.

While the examples of the truth "You reap what you sow" in this chapter have focused on negative reaping and sowing, the flip side of this truth is equally true: Each of us can sow positive thoughts and actions and can reap the healthy consequences of having done so. A person can sow healthy exercise habits that become so entrenched he or she will continue to exercise and reap physical health throughout his or her adult life. The original size of the healthy "seed" sown may be small, yet we can continue, through personal choice, to keep nurturing that seed until it grows large and produces highly positive benefits in our lives. In this light, we can also be our own best friend.

People can sow truth in their minds over the years and reap tremendous emotional benefits. That is the central theme of this book—that truth produces health in a "reap what you sow" manner. The challenge of truth, though, is to make sure it is sown properly and watered long enough to bear its reward.

USING TRUTH SERUM

In chapters 2, 3, 5 and 9, I challenged you to make broader use of your TRUTH journal. I now want to do that once more, but in a way you might not expect. This time, I want you to go back in time.

Perhaps you have one struggle in your life that you feel is more of a problem than anything else you are currently dealing with. I'd like you to sit down with your journal and make some notes as to when you believe this problem first started to get a toehold on your life. Next, add some notes about how the problem progressed, what you have done in the past to try to come to grips with it and why those efforts may not have worked well enough to please you. After that, write down ways in which you are still manifesting behavior or carrying thoughts today related to this problem.

Once your journal entries are complete, put your problem through the TRUTH system. Examine how your emotions are tied to it, what you perceive the "truth" of it to be, and how you can begin to cope with it in an emotionally healthy manner.

If this exercise proves too much for you, or if any challenge in the preceding chapters has seemed too difficult for you, let me encourage you to seek out competent counseling. Efforts to know, believe, and practice truth on your own are fine up to a point, but many people could use some professional input on the matter.

Visit a number of counselors for a single session to check them out. Ask them what they think the primary truths for emotional health are. See if they can articulate the importance of truth in building an emotionally healthy life. Then choose the best person.

With competent counseling, you can be helped to break through your defenses and see what the truth really is. You don't have to stay in darkness about the lies you believe and how they have been hurting your life. Finding a competent, professional "guide" to help you discover the truth is an extremely wise move on your part.

Additionally, let me recommend that you attend seminars and lectures on emotional health. This can help you in your efforts to get different viewpoints on an issue so that you can refine your own views over time. There are literally hundreds of seminars being offered at clinics, college campuses, hospitals, Red Cross buildings, and social service offices. Go hear what the leading experts have to say and use that information to challenge your own thinking on truth and emotional health.

PART THREE

■

DOING THE

TRUTH,

FINDING

ULTIMATE

TRUTH

CHAPTER 14

∎

How to Use the Truth to Create Emotional Health

Let us train our minds to desire
what the situation demands.
　　　　　　　　—Seneca

I n the first chapter of this book, I stated that dedication to truth was the main requirement for emotional health. In the dozen chapters that followed, I explored what I believed to be twelve of the most important truths available to help us lead an emotionally healthy life. In each of those chapters you were given a way to put your newfound knowledge to work, such as keeping a TRUTH journal, responding to a questionnaire, or doing additional reading. In this chapter, I want to provide a broader overview of the most important elements of dedication to the truth and also present you with a list of additional truths you can examine on your own. You will be able to use what you have learned in this book to write your own sequel to *The Truths We Must Believe*.

If you've completed the exercises in the previous chapters, you have developed many new truth discovery skills by now. Just because this book is drawing to a close, however, does not mean that you need those skills any less. You don't want to be like the person who hears a lecture on how to manage finances, tries out what he has learned for a short time, but doesn't keep up with it. As M. C. Richards once put it, "Let no one be deluded that a knowledge of the path can substitute for putting one foot in front of the other."

Let's talk a little more, in this chapter, about how to put "one foot in front of the other" with regard to discovering and facing the truth.

THREE FOOTSTEPS OF TRUTH

Broadly speaking, there are three important steps involved in using the truth to enhance emotional health: (1) knowing, (2) believing, and (3) doing the truth. I briefly want to discuss each step and then provide you with numerous ways you can "step" boldly.

As simple as it may sound, the first "footstep" toward using the truth for emotional health is to *know* the truth. By knowing the truth, I mean that you have discovered something to be true and have mentally acknowledged it as such. Many times in my work as a psychologist, this step may have already been accomplished to some degree by a new patient before he or she ever came in for counseling. Then again, it may be that the patient will know and believe one or two of the basic truths but not any others.

A patient may come for counseling and know that "To err is human" but not know that "The virtue lies in the struggle, not the prize" or "What should have happened did." This person knows the truth, but not as fully as he or she needs to. This individual has knowledge gaps that need to be filled in with additional truth.

The second "footstep" toward using the truth to enhance emotional health is to *believe* the truth. I am talking here about going from "head" knowledge of the truth to having real confidence and trust in the truth as something valid—confidence you would be willing to act on. A lot of us have problems with this step of truth. Many of us acknowledge the truth, but we don't have confidence in it.

A patient may come in for counseling mentally knowing that she can't have everyone's love and approval, yet she'll still be out there seeking it each day. She knows the truth, but she doesn't believe it. Thus, the truth she knows isn't doing her any good because she has not put her confidence or trust in it. It is like knowing that putting the car key into the ignition and turning it will start your car yet not believing it enough to do it. You'll just sit there and go nowhere.

The third and final "footstep" toward using the truth to enhance emotional health is to *do* the truth. Here, the truth is put actively to use. You don't just rest on the fact that you know the truth or really believe it to be true, you actually act on the truth.

In the earlier example concerning your car key, to do the truth would mean to put the key into the ignition and turn it. "Doing" the truth "Your childhood isn't over" would mean getting into therapy to explore how unresolved issues from the past are still influencing your adult life. "Doing" the truth "You don't have to" would mean choosing not to do some things that you feel you "have to" do. In this third step you'll be taking the truth and proving that it is true through action.

What I often see in my counseling practice, and in life in general, is a tendency for people to have some knowledge of truth but very little true belief in it or willingness to put it to use. In other words, a lot of us are "head smart" but it stops right there. What knowledge we have of the truth isn't very deeply watered with the experience of acting on it, thus the root system supporting that truth is shallow. The harsh winds of life often come blowing through and the truth can get uprooted pretty easily in many of us.

Far too many of us seem content just to know the truth. It's like we are college students spending the rest of our lives taking class after class but never going out and getting a job in which we can put our training to use. Fear of failure may be one of the reasons we settle here, but we end up failing miserably if we allow the fear of failure to keep us from going out and trying to apply what we know. We can't afford just to go from self-help book to self-help book, counselor to counselor, theologian to theologian asking questions about the truth but refusing to put what we know into practice. Our knowledge of truth will end up miles ahead of our application of it.

Oftentimes, when a person knows the truth but isn't using it, there is a deeper, erroneous belief controlling the situation. That deeper belief is usually some kind of half-truth or may even be a bold-faced lie, but it nevertheless is what the person is really believing and acting on. For example, a person may mentally know that life is difficult but hold a deeper, stronger belief that life should be easy, and act accordingly. The person's "head knowledge" is on the right path, but his deeper path is being controlled by some version of a lie. Thus, in spite of knowing that life is difficult, he keeps avoiding difficulty in life and fusses and whines whenever he can't.

You have truly dedicated yourself to a truth when you have come to *know, believe,* and *do* that truth. Let me give you some examples. You have truly dedicated yourself to the truth "You are going to die" when you have mentally acknowledged that this is true and you've put your trust in it as true and you, as a result of this, are out there on the planet living life with fullness and zest. You have truly dedicated yourself to the truth "You are not entitled" when you have acknowledged that as being true, have trusted it as being true, and have replaced your expectations of others with your wants and desires. You have truly dedicated yourself to the truth "You reap what you sow" when you know it to be truth, have deep trust in its being true, and are sowing healthy actions so you can reap the good rewards these actions bring.

In light of this, I think you can see just how demanding the truth really is. It isn't enough to just know the truth. Most of us seem to think that is enough, so we become "knowledge junkies." The truth asks for much more than that.

As I write these words, I feel their sting. In many ways, I, too, am a knowledge junkie, going from knowing one truth to knowing another and not always doing the hard work of making sure I believe or practice those truths. In my own life, I have not been fully dedicated to the truth and have paid the emotional price for it on occasion. I don't say this to discourage you, but just to let you know I face the same difficult struggle to dedicate myself to truth that you do. Dedication to the truth is difficult for everyone, person like me who dares to write a book about it.

The three "footsteps" of truth are *knowing* (mentally acknowledging the truth), *believing* (having confidence and trust in the truth) and *doing* (putting truth into action). All three are required for your life to be emotionally healthy. To help you in your efforts to know, believe, and do the truth, I have created the Thirty Day TRUTH Program (chapter 16). Commit yourself to following the program from Day 1 through Day 30. The benefits will pleasantly surprise you. Remember, no pain, no gain.

WRITING YOUR OWN SEQUEL

As promised, I will end this chapter by providing you with a list of truths that can be added to "Thurman's Top Twelve Truths for Emotional Health." I want you to examine them. Use your TRUTH journal to record how they affect your life on a day-to-day basis. Search other books for information that may have a bearing on your understanding of these additional truths. Compare the truths on this list to the twelve truths we examined in this book and decide how they are similar, different, compatible, innovative, or unique. Put your training to use and continue to grow.

Additional Truths to Study
1. You can run, but you can't hide.
2. Things aren't always what they seem to be.
3. Process is more important than product.
4. You train people to treat you the way they do.
5. Most of our problems never happen.
6. You tend to get what you expect.

7. Contentment begins with being satisfied with little.
8. Your life is turning out just as you want it to.
9. You can't have it all.
10. Good things come to those who wait.

CHAPTER 15

■

Is There an Ultimate Source of Truth?

Keep one thing in view forever—the truth; and if you do this, though it may seem to lead you away from the opinion of men, it will assuredly conduct you to the throne of God.

—Horace Mann

Truth is the name of the game when it comes to being an emotionally healthy person. Without truth, there is no emotional health. With truth, emotional health is an achievable reality. Certain truths, such as the twelve I have chosen to discuss in this book, play a more significant role in creating emotional health than others. Thus, these truths especially demand our understanding and use.

Yet, as I close this book, a critically important question remains to be answered: Is there an ultimate source of truth? If you don't mind my taking a crack at it, I'd like to give you my answer to that question by taking you back into my counseling office one final time.

WHERE DOES TRUTH COME FROM?

Do you remember my patient, Bill, from chapter 1? When I first introduced you to him, he was struggling with job stress, guilt over how he had handled a situation involving his son, and anger toward his wife concerning pressure she was putting on him to buy a new home. I attempted to help Bill with his problems by encouraging him to find and use the truth in each situation that was bothering him.

Bill worked pretty hard in therapy to dedicate himself to the truth. Certain truths were especially important in helping Bill resolve his emotional conflicts. We talked frequently about the truth "To err is human" in an effort to help him overcome his intolerance for personal mistakes. We spent a number of sessions on the truth "You don't have to" to help Bill overcome the erroneous notion that he had to do what people wanted him to do, like buy a new home when he knew it wasn't the best move at that time. Finally, we explored the truth "Your childhood isn't over" to help Bill overcome some unresolved hurts from his childhood that were helping to cause his overly strong need to please everyone and his perfectionistic tendencies.

As our work together neared completion, Bill and I turned our attention to the focus of this chapter: Is there an ultimate source of truth? Here is how it went.

"Dr. Thurman, I feel like I've made a lot of progress in therapy. All my problems haven't disappeared, but I'm a lot less driven to please everyone, much more accepting of myself and the mistakes I make, and freer from the guilt I felt over what happened with my son."

"You've worked hard to face the truth and apply it to your life, Bill. Your efforts have paid off nicely. I couldn't be happier about the progress you've made."

"There is something bothering me, though."

"What's that?"

"Well, you and I have worked diligently on the truth, and there is no doubt but what it has paid dividends. But outside of just using common sense or relying on trained professionals like yourself to help me, how can I really know what the truth is?"

"That's a very good question, Bill. I have struggled with that same issue in my life."

"How did you resolve it?"

"Well, I know counselors are supposed to avoid pushing their personal views on their patients, but I would like to answer your question honestly and directly."

"Good. I'd like to hear what you think."

"Well, I realized somewhere along the way that neither my own reasoning abilities nor other people's were very reliable ways of knowing what the truth is. What people have called 'truth' throughout history changes too much, as have my own notions of truth."

"Are you saying you don't really trust yourself or other people to know what's true?"

"Yes, I am. I know that sounds a little cynical, maybe even paranoid. But human beings don't strike me as a very good source of truth. As much as we might want to trust human reason or human intelligence as a way to discern truth, it often falls short. Sometimes it fails miserably. Some of the worst evils ever committed by mankind have been done in the name of 'truth.' So, no, I don't trust myself or others for the truth."

"So, who do you trust to help you know the truth?"

"God."

"That simple, huh?"

"That simple."

"Why? I mean, how do you know he even exists, much less that he can help you with truth?"

"The life of Jesus Christ answered that for me."

"What do you mean?"

"Well, while there have been a number of great thinkers throughout history who had a lot of valuable things to say about life, Christ was different."

"How?"

"He didn't claim to just know a lot of truth. He claimed to *be* truth."

"He equated himself with truth?"

"Yes. He made no distinction between himself and truth. That claim either made him the greatest lunatic of all time or who he said he was—God in human form."

"Why didn't it mean he was a lunatic? After all, that is one bold, arrogant claim."

"Not if it is true, and in Christ's case I believe it was. I think he proved his claim a number of ways."

"How?"

"First, he lived a morally perfect life. That alone made him different. No one had ever done that before, nor has anyone done it since. Second, he performed a number of miracles during his time on earth, thirty-five of which were recorded in the Bible. No human being could have done the things he did."

"Like walk on water, turn water into wine, and give sight to the blind?"

"Exactly. That also made him different and substantiated his claims as far as I'm concerned. But he did something even more miraculous than perform miracles. He came back from the dead, which he predicted he would do. I have never seen anyone pull that off either."

"Neither have I. So you are saying that not only did he make the claim to be God and truth in human form, but he backed it up?"

"Yes. To me, all that he did is a pretty impressive resume for the title of 'God' that he claimed. But the evidence supporting his claim to be God goes even further than his sinlessness, the miracles he performed, and his return from the grave."

"What else?"

"Changed lives."

"What do you mean?"

"I have seen people significantly changed because of their belief in Christ. That is the modern-day miracle that he keeps performing, even though he is no longer here in a physical body. He helps bring about personal change in people's lives that is truly miraculous. I have seen alcoholics quit drinking, rageaholics quit raging, selfish people learn to have concern for others, and numerous other changes take place in people's lives because of their commitment to Christ as the ruler of their lives."

"Isn't that a lot of religious hocus-pocus? How do you know these people didn't change for some other reason? How do you know they changed because of their relationship with Christ?"

"I can't categorically prove to you that these changes weren't due to other factors, but the view I have had of these changes in people's lives tells me a supernatural force was at work bringing the change about, not some human effort alone doing the trick."

"So you put a lot of stock in Christ and what he had to say about the truth?"

"Yes, I do. It dictated the way I worked with you."

"What?"

"My work with you has been based on truths straight from God, right out of the Bible."*

"You mean to tell me that our work together has been based on what the Bible says?"

"Yes."

"Give me some examples."

"O.K. One of the basic principles we worked on together is the idea that how you think dictates how you react. That comes out of Proverbs 23:7 where it says, "As a man thinketh, so is he." That statement basically means that what you tell yourself about the things that happen to you will determine how well you handle them. You were telling yourself a number of lies about things going on in your life, and you were paying a high price emotionally for having done so. When you started seeing the truth and using it to deal with your problems, you became much more emotionally healthy."

"So the Bible teaches that what we tell ourselves basically dictates how well we handle things?"

"Yes, and it places utmost importance on truth as the 'eyewear' through which we need to see life."

"What else about our work together came out of the Bible?"

"The specific truths I taught you all come from the Bible."

"You're kidding!"

"No, not at all."

---

* For more specific verses relating to the twelve truths discussed in this book and to truth, in general, see Appendices A and B.

"Give me some examples."

"We worked on 'To err is human,' right?"

"Yes."

"That is the human way of saying what the Bible is talking about in passages like Romans 3:23, where it says, 'For all have sinned and fall short of the glory of God' and 1 John 1:8, where it says, 'If we claim to be without sin, we deceive ourselves and the truth is not in us.' The Bible even teaches that it is our natural tendency to behave in self-centered and self-destructive ways. One verse that captures this pretty well is Proverbs 14:12. It says, 'There is a way that seems right to a man, but in the end it leads to death.' "*

"So the Bible teaches that everyone messes up and that making mistakes is an inherent part of being a human being."

"Yes, it does."

"What other truths that we worked on came out of the Bible?"

"Well, we also worked on 'You don't have to.' That truth is taught in the Bible as 'free will.' The Bible teaches that God gave us free will and that we can do what we want to, for better or for worse. We don't have to do anything if we don't want to. That is why I pushed you to see that you were free not to buy a new home if you didn't feel it was right, even though your wife might not like it. You came in acting like you had no free will, and I just tried to remind you that you do."

"O.K., but what about the childhood stuff? Where does the Bible teach about the importance of early childhood?"

* Verses are from NIV.

"Well, that is a little bit more of a stretch, but I think it is in there. The Bible emphasizes the importance of truth, as I have already mentioned. Truth sets people free. Christ was primarily interested in setting people free from the bondage of sin via the truth of who he was and the importance of turning our lives over to him. But I believe the truth also sets us free in other ways. I believe the truth sets us free from unnecessary emotional suffering."

"What does that have to do with our childhood?"

"Childhood is where your view of reality is first formed. You learn ways to think and reason in childhood that, for better or for worse, impact the rest of your life if they are never brought to light and challenged. In Deuteronomy it talks about training children in the truth so they won't leave it later on in their lives. The flip side of that is that when children are trained up in lies and distorted ways of thinking it will be hard for them to let go of these ways of thinking later on. I believe it is critically important to spend constructive time looking back into childhood experiences and teachings to see how they shaped our view of reality. The Bible teaches in 1 Corinthians that it is important to discard 'childish' thoughts and ways of reasoning that keep you from functioning as an adult. It is hard to know what to discard unless you look back in time to find what you were taught in the first place."

"What is an example of a childish way of thinking that we need to discard as adults?"

"Children tend to think that everything that happens to them is somehow their fault. We call it 'egocentric' thinking. If a parent yells at a child, the child thinks he made the parent yell at him. This, in turn, leads the child to feeling guilty, anxious, and even depressed over things he really had nothing to do with. As adults, we often still think egocentrically about things. Someone treats us badly as an adult, and we often wonder what we did wrong. We often feel like we are responsible for how people treat us. That is a faulty way of thinking left over from child-hood that needs to be replaced with the truth. The truth is, I am not responsible for other people's ac-tions or feelings. That truth frees me up to live a more mature, emotionally healthy life."

"So our childhood is where we first get pro-grammed how to think. Sometimes the programming is true, sometimes the programming is false. The true programming we keep, the false programming we try to erase and replace with truth."

"You got it."

"What else do you have up your sleeve about all this?"

"Well, I do have a final curve ball that I want to throw your way."

"I figured you did. Give me your best pitch."

"Human effort alone to know the truth in any com-plete way is doomed to fail. We bring our finiteness and fallenness into the effort, and it ends up costing us a clear view of reality. God, on the other hand, brings neither finiteness nor fallenness into the issue of truth. He is the ultimate source of all truth, and we need him to know truth completely, for eternal life and emotional health."

"You're saying I need to take a serious look at God as my source of truth."

"Yes, I believe you do. Without God, there is no ultimate truth, no lasting power to access truth, and no eternal life. That isn't me talking. That is God talking."

"Well, if God is truth, why do people who claim to believe in God seem as messed up as anyone else? I would think that with God on their side to help them know and do the truth they would be the healthiest, most mature group of all."

"I think that is the way it is supposed to work, Bill, but people who believe in God can fall into just as many distorted ideas and beliefs as anybody else if they don't dedicate themselves on a consistent basis to truth. Saying you believe in God and actually listening to him and doing things his way, day by day, are two completely different things. There are a lot of people in the former group, seemingly few in the latter."

"So the bottom line to the whole truth issue is God."

"Yes, he's the bottom line. What he inspired people to write in the Bible was his way of telling us the ultimate truths we need to know for how to live our lives. His visit to earth was an effort to put the final exclamation point on who he is and how he feels toward us. God owns the truth, and the Bible is his 'Owner's Manual' that he wants us to study so we can know how we are supposed to live."

"So there's the answer to my question. You can know truth by pursuing God and studying the book he wrote on truth."

"Yes. How does all that sound to you?"

"Like a lot to think seriously about."

WHAT ABOUT YOU?

I want to make the same challenge to you that I made to Bill. I want to challenge you to take a serious look at who your source of truth is. Are you relying on human reason and understanding to discern truth, or are you relying on the ultimate source of truth: God. If you are looking for the truth, he is it. Don't keep looking in places that can't ultimately satisfy you. Don't listen to your own common sense. Don't listen to the "experts." Listen to who wrote the book on truth: God.

If you already believe in God, let me challenge you by suggesting that you may not be listening much better than the nonbeliever to what God is trying to say to you. You may know God is truth but still be listening to your own thoughts or somebody else's as your real source of truth. God's thoughts have to become ours or we believers will not be any healthier or more mature than those who don't believe in God. If we aren't healthier or more mature, why would the nonbeliever be interested in who we have dedicated our lives to?

FINAL THOUGHTS

Psalm 119:30 says, "I have chosen the way of truth." That is what I want for you—to choose the way of truth as the basis for your life. The way of truth pays emotional health dividends, that is certain. But, more importantly, the way of truth takes you to God, the source of all truth and eternal life. The way of truth provides it all—peace and contentment here on earth that go beyond understanding, and eternal bliss in heaven that we can't even begin to grasp. Choose the way of truth and have it all.

CHAPTER 16

■

The Thirty Day TRUTH Program

This thirty-day program will help you get started in your efforts to use the truth so you can become more emotionally healthy. Please keep in mind that this program is just a way to get started, not a cure for the emotional problems that may be bothering you. You will need to practice the truths you have learned over and over again in order for them to help you significantly in overcoming the emotional struggles you have. There are no quick fixes on the road to emotional health, so please give the truth time to help you.

DAY 1

In order to discover the lies you will need to focus on during the thirty days of the program, take the Lie Questionnaire below. Make sure your response to each statement reflects how you really think, not how you suspect you "should" think. Try to avoid using the neutral ("4") response. If you are confused about what a given statement means, you may want to read the section in my book *The Lies We Believe* that discusses that particular lie.

Once you have responded to all thirty statements,

go back through the questionnaire and circle all the statements you gave a rating of 5, 6, or 7. These are the lies that are plaguing your thought life and are making you emotionally miserable.

CHART

| 1 | 2 | 3 | 4 | 5 | 6 | 7 |

Strongly Disagree   Neutral   Strongly Agree

Self Lies:

_____ 1. I must be perfect.

_____ 2. I must have everyone's love and approval.

_____ 3. It is easier to avoid my problems than to face them.

_____ 4. Things have to go my way for me to be happy.

_____ 5. My unhappiness is externally caused.

Worldly Lies:

_____ 6. I can have it all.

_____ 7. I am only as good as what I do.

_____ 8. Life should be easy.

_____ 9. Life should be fair.

_____ 10. I should not have to wait for what I want.

_____ 11. People are basically good.

Marital Lies:

_____ 12. My marriage problems are my spouse's fault.

_____ 13. If my marriage takes hard work, my spouse and I must not be right for each other.

_____ 14. My spouse should meet all my needs.

_____ 15. My spouse owes me for what I have done for him or her.

_____ 16. I should not have to change who I am in order to make my marriage better.

_____ 17. My spouse should be like me.

Distortion Lies:

——————— 18. I often make mountains out of molehills.

——————— 19. I often take things personally.

——————— 20. Things are black and white to me.

——————— 21. I often miss the forest for the trees.

——————— 22. The past predicts the future.

——————— 23. I often reason things out with my feelings rather than with the facts.

Religious Lies:

——————— 24. God's love can be earned.

——————— 25. God hates the sin and the sinner.

——————— 26. Because I am a Christian, God will protect me from pain and suffering.

——————— 27. All of my problems are caused by my sins.

——————— 28. It is my Christian duty to meet all the needs of others.

——————— 29. Painful emotions such as anger, depression, and anxiety are signs that my faith in God is weak.

——————— 30. God can't use me unless I am spiritually strong.

DAYS 2–8

Track the lies you believe for the next seven days. To do this, I want you to keep a journal and make as many entries as you can using the first three letters of the TRUTH system. For seven days, write down the trigger events (T's) you encounter and your unhealthy responses (U's) and, then, try to determine which lie or lies (R's) from the Lie Questionnaire may have caused the unhealthy responses.

For example, let's say you wait for ten minutes in a line at a fast-food restaurant to purchase your lunch, only to be told when you get to the counter that the restaurant is out of what you wanted to order. This is the trigger event *(T)*.

Let's also say that you become extremely angry and that you verbally lay into the counter person who told you the bad news. This is the unhealthy response *(U)*. Now, figure out which lie or lies may have caused your overreaction. In this situation, you may have told yourself, "Life should be easy" or "Things have to go my way for me to be happy" or "I shouldn't have to wait for what I want" or "My happiness is externally caused."

You may also have made a mountain out of a mole-hill or taken the situation personally, as if it were meant for you alone. Maybe you told yourself all these lies about the same event. Whatever lies you told yourself, write them in your journal right after the trigger event *(T)* and right before the healthy response *(H)*.

In keeping this journal, you may want to make entries in the following manner:

(T)rigger Event: Waited in a long line to get lunch; found out restaurant didn't have what I wanted.
(R)eflection/Lies: "Life should be easier and fairer than this. What is wrong with these incompetent idiots? They are making me extremely angry. I bet I'm the only one to whom this has happened today. This is really awful!"
(U)nhealthy Response: Extreme anger. Yelled at the person behind the counter. Let this episode ruin my whole day.

Dedicate yourself to this task for seven days. Keep your journal with you at all times and write down the trigger events (T's), the reflections/lies (R's) and the unhealthy responses (U's) in the order they happen. If you can't write them down at the moment they happen, try to write them afterward, as soon as you possibly can.

DAY 9

Today, you will determine the five lies you most often tell yourself and pay specific attention to those throughout the rest of the thirty days.

You can do this by going back through all the "TRU" entries you made and adding up how often each lie appears. You will probably discover that you tell yourself a lot of different lies but that certain lies show up more frequently than others.

From your tabulation, write down the five lies you tell yourself most often. These five lies are dominating your thought life and are probably causing the most damage to your emotional well-being.

DAY 10

Take each of the five lies you have identified and write a brief paragraph about why each is a lie and why you are better off not believing any of them. In other words, write a paragraph describing the truth about each lie. Let me show you how I would write about one of the lies that plagues me: "I must have everyone's love and approval":

THE LIE: "I Must Have Everyone's Approval"

I have never met anyone who had everyone's love and approval, nor have I, myself, ever had everyone's love

*and approval. So, on that basis alone, I know that the
need for everyone's approval is misguided. Plus, there are
certain things about me (and everyone else) that are not
worth loving or approving. We all have certain
deficiencies and weaknesses that other people simply
won't like because they just are not likable.*

*Besides, if everyone did approve of me, that would
mean that someone would approve of me whom I don't
like or approve of. That isn't something I really want. I
really don't want or need to be liked by people whom I
don't respect or like.*

*Finally, it takes too much energy to try to get
everyone's approval. It simply wears me out and makes
me too anxious. It is better to simply go after the love
and approval of certain people I am close to and respect
and let the approval of others be something less
consequential. Outside of my family members, my best
friends, and certain professional colleagues, if I can get
the love and approval of others, that will be fine. If I
don't, that needs to be fine also.*

Take each of the "top five" lies you believe and do
something similar to what I have done above. Use
anything about reality that you can find to argue
against the lies you tell yourself. Get as practical as
you can get in your writing about why these lies are
lies and how they are destroying your emotional life.

DAYS 11–17

Challenge your lies with the truth using all the letters
of the TRUTH system for the next seven days. As you
did during days 2–8, make journal entries on the trigger events (T), reflections/lies (R), and unhealthy re-

sponses (U), but this time I want you to fight the lies you told yourself at "R" with the truth at the second "T." Try to use as many of the truths discussed in this book as you can to challenge your lies. Note if there are any changes in your physiological, emotional, and behavioral reactions to the initial trigger event at "H" (healthy response).

To help you with this assignment, an example of a situation analyzed with the TRUTH system is given below:

(T)rigger Event: A close friend starts spending a lot of time with a new friend whom he/she has met. The close friend hardly calls anymore as his/her new friend becomes a "best" friend.

(R)eflection/Lie: "You can't trust anybody to be a true friend. That person never really cared about me in the first place. My friend owed me more loyalty than this. He/she was only using me until a better friendship came along. I will never find another person to be a close friend. I'll never get over this. I'm not good enough to keep or find friends. Life really stinks."

(U)nhealthy Response: Strong feelings of hurt, rejection, depression; isolation from others; overeating; overreacting with anger toward family members.

(T)ruth: "Understandably, my close friend's actions hurt, but the fact that he/she is spending more time with someone else doesn't mean I'm not worthwhile or a good friend. I'm not entitled to perfect loyalty and kindness from even my closest friend. I know that friendships can change, even end, but that doesn't mean that my life has to be miserable. I

don't have to spend the rest of my days bemoaning what happened. Life can be difficult, and this is one version of it. I can let my friend know how I feel about what he/she has done and see what his/her reaction is. Maybe my friend will still want to be my friend. Maybe the friendship can still go on in some enjoyable manner. I'll do what I can to find out. If the other person doesn't want to be my friend any longer, it will have been worth the effort to find out rather than just let the friendship die without any effort on my part. If I've lost a friend, I will let it hurt appropriately, but not let it crush me. There are other friendships to be found and enjoyed.''

(H)ealthy Response: Some decrease in feelings of hurt, rejection, and depression; still isolated from others some; still overeating; less anger toward family; some feelings of optimism that the situation can be dealt with in a constructive manner.

As you use the TRUTH system for the next seven days, you may notice that the truth helps some but doesn't eliminate all the unhealthy feelings and responses you initially gave the trigger event. The truth about the *truth* is that you need a great deal of practice applying it before you can overcome telling yourself some of the lies you have been for years. Don't give up on telling yourself the truth just because the emotional dividends aren't immediate. You have to stick with the truth if you want to gain the emotional dividends it can yield.

DAY 18

Record as many trigger events from the past six months of your life as you can remember. Then, write beside each event any of the twelve truths discussed in this book that would apply to the event and explain how they apply. To help you get started, let me show you how this assignment might look:

Trigger Event: *I received a ticket for speeding.*

Truths that Apply:

A. "To err is human." I made a mistake. It isn't the first time and it won't be the last. Everyone messes up now and then.

B. "What should have happened did." Given that I was speeding and breaking the law, it was appropriate for me to be issued a ticket. It doesn't make sense for me to be mad at the police officer for my choice to speed. The officer was just doing a job.

C. "You don't have to." I don't have to obey the speed limit, but not doing so can lead to getting ticketed as I did. So maybe I'd better slow down on the highway from now on. I also don't have to pay the ticket, but I think it is wise to obey the law. I'm free to do whatever I want, but not paying the ticket will only make things worse for me.

D. "Life is difficult." Life sometimes has unpleasant things in store for us, such as getting a speeding ticket.

E. "You reap what you sow." In this case, my life became more difficult because I chose to speed and I got caught. I reaped what I had sown. If I don't want tickets in the future, I'll need to slow down.

Trigger Event: My parents became furious when I decided that this year our family would celebrate the holidays at our home instead of at their home.

Truths that Apply:

A. "You can't please everyone." It is impossible to keep everyone happy with me, especially during the holidays. No matter what I would have done, someone would have been disappointed in me. My parents are now mad because we didn't go to see them, but my spouse and children would not have had as enjoyable a holiday season if we had gone. I made the best decision I could and it's my parents who don't care to understand that.

B. "You don't have to." I don't have to take my family to see my parents each holiday season, even if it means my parents will be hurt and angry over it. I don't have to do what they want me to do.

C. "Your childhood isn't over." My desire to please my parents is still strong, probably a leftover emotional need from childhood. I always wanted to please them as I grew up, and I find myself wanting to please them even now that I have my own family. Childhood feelings and issues die hard. I can still feel five years old when dealing with my parents and I still often feel a need for their approval.

D. "The virtue lies in the struggle, not the prize." My efforts to grow up and learn to be independent of my parents' approval are the important things, not whether or not they understand. I care about their feelings, but it isn't healthy for me or them if I am controlled or manipulated by their feelings. I need to stand on my own two feet and make the decisions that I think are best for my family, even if my parents sometimes get angry at me.

Trigger Event: My spouse and I had a horrible knock-down drag-out fight.

Truths that Apply:

A. "To err is human." Even though this was a pretty big error, this kind of thing happens in marriages. We made a mistake by allowing ourselves to get that angry at each other—a serious mistake! We proved our humanness in the process.

B. "What should have happened did." Given that we didn't really listen to each other or try to find a viable compromise that would work for both of us on the issue, a horrible fight like the one we had is what often happens between couples. We did not practice the things it takes to argue constructively, so the fight turned out to be destructive just like it "should" have.

C. "There is no gain without pain." Painful fights like the one we had are oftentimes the springboard to increased efforts to get along better. We can use the pain we went through to gain insight into what it is about our communication styles that gets us in trouble. We can come away from this with something good if we try hard enough.

D. "Your childhood isn't over." Our fight was a lot like the ones both sets of our parents used to have all the time in their marriages. Unfortunately, my spouse and I learned how to argue by watching our parents. We learned a lot of bad communication habits during our childhood and we're bringing these bad habits into our own marriage. Our

marriage is sometimes, if not oftentimes, an unconscious "playing out" of things we observed or
learned during childhood.

E. "Life is difficult." Having a healthy marriage
is a difficult thing to achieve. Any marriage takes
hard work. Life is difficult for a lot of reasons, the
challenges of having a healthy marriage being one
of them. We can realistically expect our marriage to
be difficult work, but it will be worth it in the long
run.

DAY 19

Take one of the twelve truths discussed in this book
and spend some specific time today meditating on it.
For example, let's say you choose to focus on the
truth, "You are not entitled."

First, spend five minutes running the phrase
through your mind. Give your mind time to get used
to hearing it said mentally over and over.

Next, say variations of this truth to yourself, such
as "I'm not entitled to love," "I'm not entitled to fairness," "I'm not entitled to get my way all the time,"
"I'm not entitled to a good living," "I'm not entitled
to kindness," "I'm not entitled to be listened to by
others" and so on. You may also want to meditate on
the idea, "It's okay to *want* _____ (love, fairness,
kindness, etc.), but it is not my birthright to have
these things."

Whatever truth you choose, the purpose of this assignment is to give your brain time to savor it. It is a
chance mentally to "work out" the truth so that it will
gain strength in your mind. The truth needs time in
your brain (as we noted at the end of chapter nine) to

establish residency and to shove aside the lies that have been there for so long.

DAY 20

Take one of the truths discussed in this book and look for life events during the day that prove it to be true. Again, using the truth "You are not entitled" as your focus, look for examples where you don't get what you feel entitled to. You might hold open a door for someone, feel entitled to a thank you, but not get one. You might be on time for lunch with a friend, feel entitled to his/her being on time as well, but wait twenty minutes before he or she shows up. You might work hard all day, feel entitled to a clean house and some peace and quiet when you arrive home, but find that the place is a mess and the kids are running wildly all over the place.

Whatever truth you choose, this assignment is aimed at helping you observe firsthand the "data" that supports the truth in question. It is one thing to have an "academic" understanding of truth. It is something else, however, to prove it true in the "laboratory of life." Collect as much evidence as you can for the truth you choose. Write down the evidence. Let what you discover deepen your understanding and appreciation for the truth.

DAY 21

Take each of the twelve truths discussed in this book and write a brief answer for each to the following question: How would my life be changed if I really believed and practiced this truth? The purpose of this assignment is to envision the changes that might take place in your life if you really allowed each truth to run your life.

DAY 22

Choose a truth from the twelve discussed in this book and act consistently with it today. Once more, let's look at the truth "You are not entitled." Spend today behaving as if you are not entitled. Hold a door open just to be kind, not to get a thank you. Be on time because you feel that is the appropriate way to be and then remind yourself that you are not entitled to the other person being on time. Go home at the end of a long day with no entitlement attitudes concerning being owed anything for how hard you worked. See if you can work on doing things because you believe in doing them or because they are right to do, not just to get something you feel entitled to. Live for one day as if you are entitled to nothing, and try to appreciate everything you get as if it were a gift that was freely given to you.

"Do" the truth today. Live your life for one day as if you believe the truth to be the truth.

DAY 23

Write a brief essay entitled, "My Source of Truth Is. . . ." In this assignment, take an honest look at what you have been relying on as your sources of truth in life. You may want to discuss such sources of "truth" as your parents, teachers, close friends, pastor, political leaders, and television news announcers. You may want to discuss in your essay whether or not you tend to let others do your thinking for you or if you do your own thinking when it comes to what the truth is. You may also want to address whether or not the things you have accepted as truth are genuinely true in your life or just something you've assumed to be true or accepted on a superficial level.

DAY 24

Address the claim of Jesus Christ that he was the truth. Do you believe what he said? If so, why? And if not, then why not? Think for yourself on this one. Don't let prejudice or the behavior of Christians get in the way of thinking about whether or not Christ was truth.

DAY 25

Take the five most frequent lies you identified on Day 9 and find verses in the Bible that argue against them. Memorize these verses. If you need some help, turn to Appendix A in my book *The Lies We Believe*, and choose from the different verses I included there.

DAYS 26–28

Use the TRUTH system to combat your five most destructive lies, but this time use the Bible verses you have learned to fight these lies. Make sure you don't just tell yourself these Bible verses are the second "T" in a matter of fact manner, as if they had little depth to them. Look more deeply into these verses. Honestly examine what they say and why they are true. Take key words from each verse and give them individual attention. Use these biblical truths to fight your lies for the next three days.

DAY 29

Read one of the four gospels (Matthew, Mark, Luke, John) and write down as many truths related to emotional and spiritual health as you can find. Once you have finished this task, go back through all the truths you wrote down and choose the five or six that you feel to be the most important. Again, commit these verses to memory and use them in your TRUTH journal to fight lies that may be creating emotional problems in your life.

DAY 30

Review all the assignments you have done during the past month. What have you learned? What improvements, if any, have there been in your emotional health? Give yourself a well-deserved pat on the back for all the hard work you have done.

Use your review of the past month to make some decisions about which assignments were the most helpful and which ones you might continue to use in your efforts to be dedicated to the truth. You may want to keep using the TRUTH system to track your lies and use the truth to fight them. You may want to keep gathering data to support the truths that you have learned in this book and from other sources. You may want to continue to study different "experts'" views of truth related to mental health by keeping up with the latest books. You will want to keep studying the Bible as a source of ultimate truth.

Whatever you do, don't let your progress slide. You have worked hard to finish the Thirty Day TRUTH Program and now you can build on top of what you have learned. Keep at it; give the truth time to do its work in your life. The payoffs will be fantastic.

NOTES

■

Chapter 1—The Absolute Necessity of Truth for an Emotionally Healthy Life

1. M. Scott Peck, M.D., *The Road Less Traveled* (New York: Touchstone, 1978), 16.

Chapter 2—To Err Is Human

1. I adapted the TRUTH system from Dr. Albert Ellis's ABCDE model, which is presented in a book he co-authored with Robert A. Harper, *A New Guide to Rational Living* (North Hollywood, CA: Wilshire, 1975). Dr. Ellis is largely responsible for the start of the self-talk movement in psychology.

Chapter 6—You Are Going to Die

1. Dr. Irvin Yalom, *Existential Psychotherapy* (New York: Basic Books, 1980).
2. Dr. Dennis E. Hensley, *How to Manage Your Time* (Anderson, IN: Warner Press, 1989), vii.
3. Russel Noyes, "Attitude Changes Following Near Death Experiences," *Psychiatry* as quoted by Dr. Irvin Yalom in *Existential Psychotherapy*.
4. Yalom, *Existential Psychotherapy*.

Chapter 7—The Virtue Lies in the Struggle, Not the Prize

1. Lord Houghton as quoted in *Stress, Sanity, and Survival* by Robert Woolfolk and Frank Richardson (New York: Simon & Schuster, 1978).
2. Donald Trump, *Survival at the Top* (New York: Random, 1990).

APPENDIX A

∎

Biblical Support for Thurman's Top Twelve Truths for Emotional Health

TRUTH #1: TO ERR IS HUMAN

To morally err is very much a part of being human. The Bible teaches that we have a sin nature. This means that it is our natural "bent" to sin (miss the moral mark). Contrast this with humanistic psychology's assumption that man is basically good, and you can see that the two views of man's nature are worlds apart.

For biblical support for the reality of the sin nature inside of all, see the passages below.

Psalm 51:5
Behold, I was brought forth in iniquity, and in sin my mother conceived me.

Romans 3:10–11
As it is written, "There is none righteous, no, not one; There is none who understands; There is none who seeks after God".

Romans 3:22–23
There is no difference; for all have sinned and fall short of the glory of God.

Romans 7:18 (NIV)

I know that nothing good lives in me, that is, in my sinful nature. For I have the desire to do what is good, but I cannot carry it out.

Romans 8:12–13

Therefore, brethren, we are debtors—not to the flesh, to live according to the flesh. For if you live according to the flesh you will die.

Galatians 5:19–21

Now other works of the flesh are evident, which are: adultery, fornication, uncleanness, licentiousness, idolatry, sorcery, hatred, contentions, jealousies, outbursts of wrath, selfish ambitions, dissensions, heresies, envy, murders, drunkenness, revelries, and the like.

TRUTH #2: WHAT SHOULD HAVE HAPPENED DID

This truth is based on the integration of a number of biblical teachings.

We have a sin nature that bends each of us toward unrighteousness:

Romans 7:18 (NIV)

I know that nothing good lives in me, that is, in my sinful nature. For I have the desire to do what is good, but I cannot carry it out.

The world is on a sinful course:

Ephesians 2:1–3

And you He made alive, who were dead in trespasses and sins, in which you once walked according to the course of this world, according to the prince of the power of the air, the spirit who now works in the sons of disobedience, among whom also we all once conducted ourselves in the lusts of our flesh, fulfilling the desires of the flesh and of the mind, and were by nature children of wrath, just as the others.

Satan is out to destroy us:
John 10:10
The thief does not come except to steal, and to kill, and to destroy.

We have a limited ability to understand these and other important realities about life:
Isaiah 55:9
For as the heavens are higher than the earth,
So are My ways higher than your ways,
And my thoughts than your thoughts.

Given these truths, it is no surprise when people do the immoral things they do. In fact, it may be more of a surprise when people don't act immorally.

Please remember that I am not saying immoral actions are "okay" or "fine." The fact that something "should have happened" given human nature does not make it right or agreeable. But I want to make it clear that with the combination of man's sin nature, Satan's efforts to destroy us, and our limited understanding, we have all the necessary "ingredients" for evil to occur. In other words, evil is no surprise given these factors. I believe we are to see evil in this light, yet fight it with all the power that God makes available to us.

TRUTH #3: YOU CAN'T PLEASE EVERYONE

The clearest biblical basis for this truth is the life of Christ. He was morally perfect, yet many people hated him.

Isaiah 53:3
"He is despised and rejected by men,
A man of sorrows,
and acquainted with grief.

And we hid, as it were, our faces from Him;
He was despised, and we did not esteem Him."

You would think that if anyone would be pleasing to everyone, he would be a morally perfect person. The life of Christ proves otherwise.

The Bible teaches not only that we can't have everyone's approval but it is not even desirable to seek it because seeking man's approval puts us at odds with God's desire that we glorify Him and that we mature as human beings. The verses that support this are:

Galatians 1:10
For do I now persuade men, or God? Or do I seek to please men? For if I still pleased men, I would not be a servant of Christ.

1 Thessalonians 2:4
But as we have been approved by God to be entrusted with the gospel, even so we speak, not as pleasing men, but God who tests our hearts.

James 4:4
Adulterers and adulteresses! Do you not know that friendship with the world is enmity with God? Whoever therefore wants to be a friend of the world makes himself an enemy of God.

God's approval is to be our focus, not the approval of man. I would be more concerned about someone who seemingly had everyone's approval than someone who didn't. After all, what kind of person would be pleasing to *everyone*? That would be one "chameleon" of a person with little firmness of beliefs and values. I'd rather stand for something and be despised or disliked than stand for nothing and be accepted by most.

TRUTH #4: YOU DON'T HAVE TO

The Bible teaches that we have free will (see the verses below), which means we are free to do whatever we want. In light of this, there are no pure "have to's" in life. We are free to go our own way in life, but there are consequences to the choices we make.

One of the important aspects of Christ's death on the cross was to set us free from the impossible burden of the "law" as the means by which to gain God's favor (see Matthew 10:8 below). The law was "You have to do _____ to please God," something that sinful man couldn't, on his own, ever do well enough. Christ's death has set us free from having to do things to merit God's favor. In response, we believers are to pursue righteousness as a way to show gratefulness and appreciation for what Christ did on the cross.

Some of the verses that support the truth "You don't have to" are:

Deuteronomy 30:19–20
"I call heaven and earth as witnesses today against you, that I have set before you life and death, blessings and cursing; therefore choose life, that both you and your descendants may live; that you may love the Lord your God, that you may obey His voice, and that you may cling to Him."

Proverbs 8:10–11
Receive my instruction, and not silver, and knowledge rather than choice gold;
For wisdom is better than rubies,
And all the things one may desire cannot be compared with her.

Proverbs 16:16
How much better it is to get wisdom than gold.

And to get understanding is to be chosen rather than silver.

Matthew 10:8

"Freely you have received, freely give."

John 7:17

"If anyone wants to do His will, he shall know concerning the doctrine, whether it is from God or whether I speak on my own authority."

Galatians 5:1 (NIV)

It is for freedom that Christ has set us free. Stand firm, then, and do not let yourselves be burdened again by a yoke of slavery.

TRUTH #5: YOU ARE GOING TO DIE

The Bible is pretty straightforward about this truth (see verses below). We are given life by God and that life will come to an end someday. The Bible also teaches that we die once, which makes reincarnation untenable. We truly "only go around once in life" according to the Bible, which is to be used as a motivation to make sure our journey through life is dedicated to important things that last rather than temporary things that please only us. We are to base our lives on God's plan, not our own.

Some of our biblical passages that teach the truth "You are going to die" are:

Psalm 89:48

What man can live and not see death?
Can he deliver his life from the power of the grave?

Ecclesiastes 3:2

A time to be born,
And a time to die

Ecclesiastes 7:2 (NIV)
It is better to go to a house of mourning than to go to a house of feasting, for death is the destiny of every man.

Hebrews 9:27
And as it is appointed for men to die once, . . .

TRUTH #6: THE VIRTUE LIES IN THE STRUGGLE, NOT THE PRIZE

The Bible teaches that we will never be perfectly moral or mature during our lives no matter how hard we try (see verses supporting the truth "To err is human"). With that in mind, I would argue that *the effort* to grow in righteousness and maturity is the virtue since the "prize" of perfect righteousness and maturity are unattainable.

The "good news" is that Christ's death on the cross took care of the problem that we can never be morally perfect. The fact that we can never live perfect moral lives has been solved through Christ's willingness to die for our sins. Those who believe in Christ and accept him as their Savior are made righteous in God's eyes through the atoning death of Christ on the cross.

The key verses that I believe support the truth "The virtue lies in the struggle, not the prize" are:

Philippians 3:12–15
Not that I have already attained, or am already perfected; but I press on, that I may lay hold of that for which Christ Jesus has also laid hold of me. Brethren, I do not count myself to have apprehended; but one thing I do, forgetting those things which are behind and reaching forward to those things which are ahead, I press toward the goal for the prize of the upward call of God in Christ Jesus. Therefore let us, as many as are mature, have this mind; and if in anything you think otherwise, God will reveal even this to you.

Hebrews 12:1–3

Therefore we also, since we are surrounded by so great a cloud of witnesses, let us lay aside every weight, and the sin which so easily ensnares us, and let us run with endurance the race that is set before us, looking unto Jesus, the author and finisher of our faith, who for the joy that was set before Him endured the cross, despising the shame, and has sat down at the right hand of the throne of God.

TRUTH #7: YOU ARE NOT ENTITLED

If the Bible teaches we were entitled to anything, it teaches we were entitled to eternity in hell for our sinfulness (Ephesians 2:4–5—"But God, who is rich in mercy, because of His great love with which He loved us, even when we were dead in trespasses, made us alive together with Christ (by grace you have been saved)"). Walking around feeling entitled to things is quite prideful and Scripture says God detests pride: "God resists the proud,/But gives grace to the humble" (James 4:6). Salvation itself is the result of God's grace, not something we earned through good behavior.

I would make the same point about human relationships. Just as we were not entitled to God's love or forgiveness (or anything else He offers), we are not entitled to these from people either. It is not our "birthright" to get our needs met by others, and to feel entitled to getting our needs met is to invite great anger and bitterness. Desiring to get our needs met and humbly trying to get them met is the more appropriate stance.

Ephesians 2:1–9

And you He made alive, who were dead in trespasses and sins, in which you once walked according to the course of this world, according to the prince of the power of the air, the spirit who now works in the sons of disobedience, among whom also we all once conducted ourselves in the lusts of our flesh, fulfilling the desires of the flesh and of the mind, and were by nature children of wrath, just as the others. But God, who is rich in mercy, because of His great love with which He loved us, even when we were dead in trespasses, made us alive together with Christ (by grace you have been saved), and raised us up together, and made us sit together in the heavenly places in Christ Jesus, that in the ages to come He might show the exceeding riches of His grace in His kindness toward us in Christ Jesus. For by grace you have been saved through faith, and that not of yourselves; it is the gift of God, not of works lest anyone should boast.

TRUTH #8: THERE IS NO GAIN WITHOUT PAIN

The idea that suffering is required to produce maturity runs throughout the Bible. The Bible clearly teaches that suffering for righteousness' sake is "good" suffering and not to be avoided. James 1:2–4 says, "Consider it pure joy, my brothers, whenever you face trials of many kinds, because you know that the testing of your faith develops perseverance. Perseverance must finish its work so that you may be mature and complete, not lacking anything" (NIV).

While we often complain about problems and the suffering they can bring, it is through painful problems that maturity can be achieved. Paying the price of personal suffering in order to mature is difficult but yields great reward. As Paul put it in Philippians 3:8, "But indeed I also count all things loss for the excellence of the knowledge of Christ Jesus my Lord, for whom I have suffered the loss of all things, and count them rubbish, that I may gain Christ."

Just as we put difficult math problems in front of our children so that they might learn important mathematical skills, life throws us difficult problems that when suffered through produce important life skills. Don't let anyone sell you a "pain free" approach to gain: They are leading you down a deadly garden path you don't want to be on.

TRUTH #9: YOUR CHILDHOOD ISN'T OVER

This truth is a little bit of a stretch, yet I feel it can be supported biblically. The Bible talks about the need for adults to put childish ways of thinking behind us (see 1 Corinthians 13:11 below), suggesting that ways of thinking and reasoning from childhood can still be in us during our adult years and interfere with our maturation. Also, there are a number of verses (see below) that talk about the importance of training up children in the truth so they won't depart from it later in life. The flip side of this would be the idea that training up children in lies and distortions would make it difficult for them to depart from those views later in life. I have certainly found this to be true in my work as a psychologist.

 While what happened to us in the past can wrongfully be used to rationalize immaturity and unrighteousness as adults, I believe the past needs to be seen as the time during which our views of God, ourselves, others, and life in general were first formed. Our beliefs formed during childhood need to be exposed, and the faulty beliefs, countered with the truth. To not do so allows childish thinking not only to run our adult lives but to ruin them. Immature beliefs are incapable of helping us be competent adults. Adults need to think like adults, not like children.

Some of the biblical verses that support the truth "Your childhood isn't over" are:

Deuteronomy 4:9
"Only take heed to yourself, and diligently keep yourself, lest you forget the things your eyes have seen, and lest they depart from your heart all the days of your life. And teach them to your children and your grandchildren."

Deuteronomy 11:18–19
"Therefore you shall lay up these words of mine in your

heart and in your soul, and bind them as a sign on your hand, and they shall be as frontlets between your eyes. You shall teach them to your children, speaking of them when you sit in your house, when you walk by the way, when you lie down, and when you rise up."

Proverbs 22:6
Train up a child in the way he should go,
And when he is old he will not depart from it.

Proverbs 29:17
Discipline your son, and he will give you peace; he will bring delight to your soul (NIV).

1 Corinthians 13:11
When I was a child, I spoke as a child, I understood as a child, I thought as a child; but when I became a man, I put away childish things.

1 Corinthians 14:20
Brothers, stop thinking like children. In regard to evil be infants, but in your thinking be adults (NIV).

Ephesians 6:4
And you, fathers, do not provoke your children to wrath, but bring them up in the training and admonition of the Lord.

Colossians 3:21
Fathers, do not provoke your children, lest they become discouraged.

TRUTH #10: EMOTIONAL PROBLEMS ARE GOOD

None of us wants to be emotionally troubled, and the ideal would be that we never experience clinically significant emotional problems. But, given our sinful nature (and everyone else's), significant emotional problems are going to occur. While we may bemoan our emotional problems, they are an important signal to us that something inside our thoughts needs correction. Thus, emotional suffering can be a springboard to growth and maturity. Emotional suffering can be "good" in that it alerts us and motivates us to change when we have gotten off course.

Another "good" aspect of emotional problems is that they enable us to empathize with others who suffer. When we go through emotional suffering, we know what it is like when others do. This allows us to offer comfort to them.

I, like you, would like to stay mentally healthy enough that I never suffer emotional problems. But given my own tendency to not listen to or practice truth, painful emotional problems will come my way. Because they signal me that I need to correct something, I can actually thank God for their important role in my life.

Some of the biblical verses that support the truth that, "Emotional problems are good" are:

Matthew 5:4
"Blessed are those who mourn,
For they shall be comforted."

2 Corinthians 1:3–4
Blessed be the God and Father of our Lord Jesus Christ, the Father of mercies and God of all comfort, who comforts us in all our tribulation, that we may be able to comfort those who are in any trouble, with the comfort with which we ourselves are comforted by God.

Romans 5:3–4
And not only that, but we also glory in tribulations, knowing that tribulation produces perseverance; and perseverance, character; and character, hope.

Romans 8:28
And we know that all things work together for good to those who love God, to those who are the called according to His purpose.

James 1:2

Consider it pure joy, my brothers, whenever you face trials of many kinds, because you know that the testing of your faith develops perseverance. Perseverance must finish its work so that you may be mature and complete, not lacking anything (NIV).

TRUTH #11: LIFE IS DIFFICULT

The Bible teaches that since the moral fall of man life has been difficult for all (see Genesis 3:17–19 below). Sin entered the world and things have been rough ever since. Perhaps the most staggering proof that life is difficult for everyone is the life of Christ. He, as co-creator of the universe with God the Father and God the Holy Spirit, found life to be difficult. You would think that if life would ease off for anyone it would ease off for the very Being who helped to create it. Birth in a smelly manger, attempts on His life, unfair attacks on His character, disloyalty by friends, beatings, and death on a cross suggest otherwise.

Biblical verses that support the truth "Life is difficult" are:

Genesis 3:17–19

Then to Adam He said, "Because you have heeded the voice of your wife, and have eaten from the tree of which I commanded you, saying,

'You shall not eat of it':
Cursed is the ground for your sake;
In toil you shall eat of it
All the days of your life.
Both thorns and thistles it shall bring forth for you,
And you shall eat the herb of the field.
In the sweat of your face you shall eat bread
Till you return to the ground,
For out of it you were taken;

> For dust you are,
> And to dust you shall return."

Ecclesiastes 1:8
All things are wearisome, more than one can say (NIV).

Ecclesiastes 2:22–23
For what has man for all his labor, and for the striving of his heart with which he has toiled under the sun? For all his days are sorrowful, and his work grievous; even in the night his heart takes no rest. This also is vanity.

Matthew 6:34
"Therefore do not worry about tomorrow, for tomorrow will worry about its own things. Sufficient for the day is its own trouble."

TRUTH #12: YOU REAP WHAT YOU SOW

The truth "You reap what you sow" shows up frequently in the Bible. According to Scripture, this principle applies both negatively and positively to our lives (see Proverbs 11:18 below). Applied to the basic focus of this book, the thoughts we sow create the life we reap. Or, as Proverbs 23:7 puts it, "As a man thinketh, so is he."

Some of the verses that support the truth "You reap what you sow" are:

Job 4:8
> Even as I have seen,
> Those who plow iniquity,
> And sow trouble reap the same.

Proverbs 11:18
> The wicked man does deceptive work,
> But to him who sows righteousness will be a sure reward.

Proverbs 22:8

He who sows iniquity will reap sorrow,
And the rod of his anger will fail.

2 Corinthians 9:6

But this I say: He who sows sparingly will also reap sparingly, and he who sows bountifully will also reap bountifully.

Galatians 6:7–8

Do not be deceived, God is not mocked; for whatever a man sows, that he will also reap. For he who sows to his flesh will of the flesh reap corruption, but he who sows to the Spirit will of the Spirit reap everlasting life.

APPENDIX B

■

Key Biblical Passages on Truth

1. TRUTH AS PROTECTION

Psalm 40:11
Do not withhold Your tender mercies from me, O Lord;
Let Your lovingkindness and Your truth continually
preserve me.

2. DEDICATION TO TRUTH

Psalm 26:3
And I have walked in Your truth.

Psalm 86:11
Teach me Your way, O Lord;
I will walk in Your truth.

Proverbs 23:23
Buy the truth, and do not sell it.

James 1:22–25
But be doers of the word, and not hearers only, deceiving
yourselves. For if anyone is a hearer of the word and not a
doer, he is like a man observing his natural face in a mirror;
for he observes himself, goes away, and immediately for-
gets what kind of man he was. But he who looks into the
perfect law of liberty and continues in it, and is not a for-

getful hearer but a doer of the work, this one will be blessed in what he does.

3. THE ABSENCE OF TRUTH IN THE WORLD

Isaiah 59:14–15
"Justice is turned back,
And righteousness stands afar off;
For truth is fallen in the street,
And equity cannot enter.
So truth fails,
And he who departs from evil makes himself a prey."

Jeremiah 7:28
"So you shall say to them, 'This is a nation that does not obey the voice of the LORD their God nor receive correction. Truth has perished and has been cut off from their mouth.' "

Jeremiah 9:5
"Everyone will deceive his neighbor,
And will not speak the truth."

Romans 1:25
[They] exchanged the truth of God for the lie, and worshiped and served the creature rather than the Creator, who is blessed forever.

2 Timothy 4:3–4
For the time will come when they will not endure sound doctrine, but according to their own desires, because they have itching ears, they will heap up for themselves teachers; and they will turn their ears away from the truth, and be turned aside to fables.

4. CHRIST'S CLAIM TO BE TRUTH

John 14:6
Jesus said to him, "I am the way, the truth, and the life. No one comes to the Father except through Me."

John 18:37
Pilate therefore said to Him, "Are You a king then?" Jesus answered, "You say rightly that I am a king. For this cause I was born, and for this cause I have come into the world, that I should bear witness to the truth. Everyone who is of the truth hears My voice."

5. CONSEQUENCES OF REJECTING TRUTH

Romans 1:18
For the wrath of God is revealed from heaven against all ungodliness and unrighteousness of men, who suppress the truth in unrighteousness.

Romans 2:8 (NIV)
But for those who are self-seeking and who reject the truth and follow evil, there will be wrath and anger.

2 Thessalonians 2:10 (NIV)
They perish because they refused to love the truth and so be saved.

2 Thessalonians 2:12
All may be condemned who did not believe the truth but had pleasure in unrighteousness.

6. CONSEQUENCES OF ACCEPTING TRUTH

Titus 1:1
Paul, a servant of God and an apostle of Jesus Christ, according to the faith of God's elect and the acknowledgment of the truth which is according to godliness.

James 1:18

Of His own will He brought us forth by the word of truth, that we might be a kind of firstfruits of His creatures.

1 Peter 1:22

Since you have purified your souls in obeying the truth through the Spirit in sincere love of the brethren, love one another fervently with a pure heart.

7. GOD THE HOLY SPIRIT GUIDING US IN TRUTH

John 15:26

"But when the Helper comes, whom I shall send to you from the Father, the Spirit of truth who proceeds from the Father, He will testify of Me."

John 16:13–15

"However, when He, the Spirit of truth, has come, He will guide you into all truth; for He will not speak on His own authority, but whatever He hears He will speak; and He will tell you things to come. He will glorify Me, for He will take of what is Mine and declare it to you. All things that the Father has are Mine. Therefore I said that He will take of Mine and declare it to you."

Galatians 5:22–23

But the fruit of the Spirit is love, joy, peace, long-suffering, kindness, goodness, faithfulness, gentleness, self-control. Against such there is no law.

8. THE ROLE OF THE BIBLE IN OUR LIVES

Psalm 119:105

Your word is a lamp to my feet
And a light to my path.

2 Timothy 3:16–17

All Scripture is given by inspiration of God, and is profitable for doctrine, for reproof, for correction, for instruction in righteousness, that the man of God may be complete, thoroughly equipped for every good work.

Hebrews 4:12

For the word of God is living and powerful, and sharper than any two-edged sword, piercing even to the division of soul and spirit, and of joints and marrow, and is a discerner of the thoughts and intents of the heart.